.L ECONOMICS

NO.   M

THE POLITICAL ECONOMY OF
CENTRAL-BANK INDEPENDENCE

SYLVESTER C. W. EIJFFINGER

AND

JAKOB DE HAAN

INTERNATIONAL FINANCE SECTION

DEPARTMENT OF ECONOMICS
PRINCETON UNIVERSITY
PRINCETON, NEW JERSEY

INTERNATIONAL FINANCE SECTION
EDITORIAL STAFF

Library of Congress Cataloging-in-Publication Data

Eijffinger, Sylvester C. W.
   The political economy of central-bank independence / Sylvester C.W. Eijffinger and Jakob De Haan.
   p. cm.—(Special papers in international economics ; no. 19)
   Includes bibliographical references.
   ISBN 0-88165-308-X (pbk.) : $11.00
   1. Banks and banking, Central. I. Haan, Jakob De. II. Title.
HG1811.E37 1996
332.1'1—dc20

96-14334
CIP

Printed in the United States of America by Princeton University Printing Services at Princeton, New Jersey

International Standard Serial Number: 0081-3559
International Standard Book Number: 0-88165-308-X
Library of Congress Catalog Card Number: 96-14334

"THE ONLY GOOD CENTRAL BANK IS ONE THAT CAN SAY
NO TO POLITICIANS"

(*The Economist*, February 10, 1990, p. 10)

PREFACE

In recent years, academics and policymakers have shown increasing interest in the independence of central banks with respect to the formulation of monetary policy. In the European Union, this interest was realized in the Treaty on European Union (Maastricht Treaty), according to which the European Central Bank will have complete autonomy in conducting the common monetary policy of the European Union. Hungary, the Czech Republic, and several other countries in Central Europe have decided on autonomy for their central banks. In most of the Anglo-Saxon countries, the issue continues to be discussed. Public debate in the United Kingdom seems to lean toward more independence for the Bank of England; the Congress in the United States continues to question the autonomy of the Federal Reserve.

This paper analyzes from various perspectives the advantages and disadvantages of central-bank independence and discusses the theoretical and empirical arguments in favor of autonomy. It reviews and criticizes generally accepted indices of central-bank independence, investigates the determinants of independence, and, ultimately, tries to decide whether or not an independent central bank is, in practice, desirable.

We wish to acknowledge a number of colleagues for their many helpful comments and suggestions on previous drafts of this paper. We are especially grateful to Onno De Beaufort Wijnholds, Helge Berger, Alex Cukierman, Paul De Grauwe, Gert-Jan Van 't Hag, Marco Hoeberichts, Lex Hoogduin, André Icard, Otmar Issing, Flip De Kam, Mervyn King, David Laidler, Manfred Neumann, Ad Van Riet, Eric Schaling, Helmut Schlesinger, Pierre Siklos, Dave Smant, Carl Walsh, Nout Wellink, Tony Yates, Jean Zwahlen, and an anonymous referee. The views expressed in the paper remain solely the responsibility of the authors, however, and should not be interpreted as reflecting the opinions of these scholars and policymakers or their institutions.

Tilburg/Groningen   Sylvester C.W. Eijffinger
May 1996   Jakob De Haan

1 INTRODUCTION

It is often argued that a high level of central-bank independence coupled with an explicit mandate that the bank aim for price stability are important institutional devices for maintaining that stability. Indeed, a number of countries have recently increased the independence of their central banks in order to raise their commitment to price stability. According to Cukierman (1995), they have done so for various reasons. First, the breakdown of institutions designed to safeguard price stability—the Bretton Woods system and the European Monetary System (EMS), for example—has led countries to search for alternatives. Second, the relative autonomy of the Bundesbank is often seen as evidence that central-bank independence can function as an effective device for assuring price stability (Germany has one of the best post–World War II inflation records among the industrial countries). Third, the Treaty on European Union (Maastricht Treaty) requires an independent central bank as a precondition for membership in the Economic and Monetary Union (EMU); price stability will be the major objective of the future European System of Central Banks (ESCB), which will consist of the European Central Bank (ECB) and the national central banks of all the member states of the European Union (EU). Fourth, after recent periods of successful stabilization, policymakers in many Latin American countries are looking for institutional arrangements that can reduce the likelihood of a return to high and persistent inflation. Fifth, the creation of independent central banks in many former socialist countries is part of a more general attempt of these countries to create the institutional framework needed for the orderly functioning of a market economy. The extensive recent literature suggesting that inflation and central-bank independence are negatively related has also, no doubt, prompted governments to consider enhancing the autonomy of their central banks. This paper critically reviews that debate.

Most authors provide no clear definition of central-bank independence. According to Friedman (1962), central-bank autonomy refers to a relation between the central bank and the government that is comparable to the relation between the judiciary and the government. The judiciary can rule only on the basis of laws provided by the legislature, and it can be forced to rule differently only through a change in the

1

law. Central-bank independence relates to three areas in which the influence of government must be either excluded or drastically curtailed (Hasse, 1990): independence in personnel matters, financial independence, and independence with respect to policy. *Personnel independence* refers to the influence the government has in appointment procedures. It is not feasible to exclude government influence completely in appointments to a public institution as important as a central bank. The level of this influence, however, may be discerned by criteria such as government representation in the governing body of the central bank and government influence in appointment procedures, terms of office, and dismissal of the governing board of the bank.

Financial independence refers to the ability given to the government to finance government expenditure either directly or indirectly through central-bank credits. Direct access to central-bank credits implies that monetary policy is subordinated to fiscal policy. Indirect access may result if the central bank is cashier to the government or if it handles the management of government debt.

Policy independence refers to the maneuvering room given to the central bank in the formulation and execution of monetary policy. As pointed out by Debelle and Fischer (1995) and Fischer (1995), it may be useful to distinguish between independence with respect to *goals* and independence with respect to *instruments*. Two related issues are important with respect to goals: the scope the central bank has to exercise its own discretion and the presence or absence of monetary stability as the central bank's primary goal. If the central bank has been assigned various goals, such as low inflation and low unemployment, it has been accorded the greatest possible scope for discretion. In that case, the central bank is independent with respect to goals, because it is free to set the final goals of monetary policy. It may, for example, decide that price stability is less important than output stability and act accordingly. If it is given either general or specific objectives with respect to price stability, however, the central banks's discretionary powers will be restricted.

To defend its goals, however, a central bank must wield effective policy instruments. A bank is independent with respect to instruments if it is free to choose the means by which to achieve its goals. It is not independent if it requires government approval to use policy instruments.[1] The Reserve Bank of New Zealand, for which the goal is precisely described in a contract with the government, is not independent with respect to

---

[1] If the central bank is obliged to finance budget deficits, moreover, it also lacks instrument independence. In this regard, financial independence and instrument independence

2

goals; it is independent with respect to instruments, however, because it chooses the methods by which to achieve its goal.

This paper uses the distinction between these aspects of independence in reviewing the literature on central-bank autonomy. It considers four issues. Chapter 2 begins with a review of the theoretical case for central-bank independence. The literature has advanced various arguments to explain why countries with relatively independent central banks may have a better inflation performance than countries in which politicians have control over the central banks. These arguments often refer to one or more specific aspects of central-bank independence. Although central-bank autonomy may improve inflation performance, it may also yield undesirable consequences in terms of lower and more volatile economic growth rates.

Chapter 3 discusses the ways in which central-bank independence has been measured and reviews four widely used indices of central-bank autonomy. These measures have been developed by Alesina (1988, 1989), Grilli, Masciandaro, and Tabellini (1991), Cukierman (1992), and Eijffinger and Schaling (1992, 1993a). Although the measures all focus on legal aspects of central-bank independence, they diverge in their rankings of central banks. The measures place different weights on the various aspects of central-bank independence, as outlined above.

Chapter 4 reviews empirical studies on the link between central-bank autonomy and economic performance. It begins by discussing the relation between central-bank independence and the level and variability of inflation, reviews the link between independence and the level and variability of economic growth, and considers whether central-bank independence reduces disinflation costs. The chapter concludes with a brief review of studies discussing the link between central-bank independence and other variables such as interest rates and government budget deficits.

Chapter 5 questions why central-bank independence varies across countries—that is, what the determinants are of central-bank independence. This issue has only recently been put on the research agenda. Chapter 6 concludes the paper.

---

are related; instrument independence is, however, much broader, because it includes also the power to determine interest rates.

2   THEORETICAL CONSIDERATIONS ON CENTRAL-BANK INDEPENDENCE

Inflation

Many observers believe that countries with independent central banks have lower levels of inflation than countries in which central banks are under the direct control of the government. Why would central-bank independence, *ceteris paribus*, yield lower rates of inflation? The literature provides three sorts of answers to this question: those based on public-choice arguments, those based on the analysis of Sargent and Wallace (1981), and those based on the time-inconsistency problem of monetary policy.

According to the "older" public-choice view, monetary authorities are exposed to strong political pressures to behave in accordance with the government's preferences.[2] Monetary tightening aggravates the budgetary position of the government. The reduction in tax income brought about by a temporary slowdown of economic activity, possibly lower receipts from "seigniorage," and the short-run increase in the interest burden on public debt all worsen the deficit. The government may therefore prefer "easy money." Indeed, some evidence exists that even the relatively independent U.S. Federal Reserve caters to the desires of the president, the Congress, or both. This evidence is based either on close inspection of the contacts between the polity and the central bank or on tests to determine whether monetary policy turns expansive before elections[3]—as predicted by Nordhaus's (1975) theory of the political business cycle (Allen, 1986)—or diverges under administrations with

[2] As Buchanan and Wagner (1977, pp. 117-118) put it: "A monetary decision maker is in a position only one stage removed from that of the directly elected politician. He will normally have been appointed to office by a politician subject to electoral testing, and he may even serve at the pleasure of the latter. It is scarcely to be expected that persons who are chosen as monetary decision makers will be the sort that are likely to take policy stances sharply contrary to those desired by their political associates, especially since these stances would also run counter to strong public opinion and media pressures. . . . 'Easy money' is also 'easy' for the monetary manager. . . ."

[3] See, for example, Akhtar and Howe (1991) and Havrilesky (1993). Havrilesky (p. 30) even argues that "the contemporary view is that the [U.S.] Administration, while granting significant leeway to the Fed, when necessary obtains the monetary policy actions that it desires."

4

different political orientation—as predicted by Hibbs's (1977) partisan theory (Alesina, 1988). At this stage, it suffices to conclude that the more independent a central bank is, the less it will be under the spell of political influences. The argument of Buchanan and Wagner relates primarily to independence with respect to personnel and policy.[4] The more influential the government is in appointing board members, the more likely it will be that the central bank pursues the kinds of policies desired by government.

A second argument to explain why central-bank independence may tear on inflation was first put forward by Sargent and Wallace (1981), who distinguish between fiscal authorities and monetary authorities. If fiscal policy is dominant, that is, if the monetary authorities cannot influence the size of the government's budget deficit, money supply becomes endogenous. If the public is no longer able or willing to absorb additional government debt, it follows from the government budget constraint that monetary authorities will be forced to finance the deficit by creating money. If, however, monetary policy is dominant, the fiscal authorities will be forced to reduce the deficit (or repudiate part of the debt). The more independent the central bank is, the less the monetary authorities can be forced to finance deficits by creating money. This argument relates to financial independence.

A third, and, indeed, the most prominent, argument for central-bank independence is based on the time-inconsistency problem (Kydland and Prescott, 1977; Calvo, 1978; Barro and Gordon, 1983). Dynamic inconsistency arises when the best plan made in the present for some future period is no longer optimal when that period actually starts. Various models have been based on this dynamic-inconsistency approach (Rogoff, 1985; Cukierman, 1992; Eijffinger and Schaling, 1993b; Schaling, 1995). In these models, the government and the public are drawn into some setting of the prisoner's dilemma. The

---

[4] Neumann (1991, p. 103) emphasizes personnel independence with respect to the governing board of the central bank: "The conditions of contract and of office would have to be set such that the appointee frees him- or herself from all former political ties or dependencies and accepts the central bank's objective of safeguarding the value of the currency as his or her professional *leitmotif*. We may call this a 'Thomas Becket' effect." Waller (1992b) develops a model for appointments to the central bank in the context of a two-party political system, in which the victor of the last election is allowed to nominate candidates, but the losing party is given the right to confirm the nominees. An interesting outcome of the model is that if society wants to minimize partisan monetary policy, it should increase the length of office of central-bank policy-board members relative to the length of the electoral interval.

models differ in their assumptions with regard to government incentives. Following McCallum (1995a), their central insights may be explained as follows. It is assumed that policymakers seek to minimize the loss function

$$L(\pi_t) = w\pi^2 + (y_t - ky_n)^2 , \qquad (1)$$

where $0 < w$ and $k > 1$, whereas output is driven by

$$y_t = y_n + \beta(\pi_t - \pi_t^e + u_t) , \qquad (2)$$

where π is inflation, π^e is expected inflation, y_t is output, y_n is the natural output, and u_t is a random shock. We assume, here, that deviations of employment from its natural level are positively related to unanticipated inflation. This follows from the existence of nominal-wage contracts in conjunction with a real wage that is normally above the market-clearing real wage. Policymakers have an objective function that assigns a positive weight to employment stimulation (for reelection considerations, for example, or for partisan reasons) and a negative weight to inflation. Policymakers minimize the loss function (equation [1]) on a period-by-period basis, taking the inflation expectations as given. This gives

$$\pi_t = \frac{\beta(k - 1)y_n}{w + \beta^2} + \frac{\beta^2}{w + \beta^2}\pi_t^e - \frac{\beta^2}{w + \beta^2}u_t . \qquad (3)$$

With rational expectations, inflation is then

$$\pi_t = \frac{\beta(k - 1)y_n}{w} - \frac{\beta^2}{w + \beta^2}u_t . \qquad (4)$$

If policymakers were to follow a rule taking into account private rational-expectational behavior, inflation would be

$$\pi_t = \frac{-\beta^2}{w + \beta^2}u_t . \qquad (5)$$

Because the same level of output pertains in both cases, the latter outcome is clearly superior. No matter what exactly causes the dynamic-inconsistency problem, the resulting rate of inflation is, in all cases, suboptimal.[5]

---

[5] Other sources of the time-inconsistency problem originate with the public finances. The dynamic inconsistency of monetary policy may first arise because of the incentives for the government to inflate change before and after the public has settled for a nominal interest rate, taking into account its expected rate of inflation. Before the public commits

Devices have therefore been suggested in the literature to reduce the inflationary bias. Barro and Gordon (1983) conclude that the best solution for the time-inconsistency problem consists of the introduction of fixed rules in monetary policy, that is, the authorities commit themselves to certain policy rules. Once uncertainty is introduced and the level of output is affected by shocks, the case becomes one for a feedback rule, in which monetary policy optimally responds to shocks. The problem with rules, however, is the absence of a higher authority to enforce a commitment. The handing-over of authority to the central bank by the political authorities may help, because it can be regarded as an act of partial commitment (Rogoff, 1985; Neumann, 1991; Cukierman, 1992, chap. 18). By delegating some of their authority to a relatively apolitical institution, politicians accept certain restrictions on their future freedom of action.[6]

The degree of central-bank independence plays a meaningful role only if the central bank puts a different emphasis on alternative policy objectives than the government. The literature points to two main differences (Cukierman, 1992, chap. 18). One relates to possible differences between the rate of time preference of political authorities and that of central banks. For various reasons, central banks are often more conservative and take a longer view of the policy process than do politicians. The other difference concerns the subjective weights in the objective function of the central bank and that of the government. It is often assumed that central bankers are more concerned about inflation than about policy goals such as the achievement of high employment levels and adequate government revenues. If monetary policy is set at the discretion of a conservative central banker, a lower average time-

---

itself, the central bank has an incentive to abstain from making inflation. After positions in government bonds have been taken, policymakers have an incentive to create inflation (Cukierman, 1992). Another source of the inconsistency problem also originates in the finances of government and may be referred to as the "revenue" or "seigniorage" motive for monetary expansion (Barro, 1983). The dynamic inconsistency of monetary policy arises in this regard because of incentives for the government to inflate change before and after the public has chosen the level of real money balances. The conclusion that the resulting rate is suboptimal generally also holds for models with incomplete information. Cukierman (1992, chap. 18), for instance, provides a model in which the public is not fully informed about the shifting objectives of the political authorities and in which there is no perfect control of information.

[6] An alternative solution to the time-inconsistency problem is reputation building (Canzoneri, 1985). Fratianni and Huang (1994) show, however, that the case of asymmetric information gives no assurance that reputation may work for the central bank in the Barro-Gordon model.

consistent inflation rate will result.[7] The foregoing analysis makes it clear that this argument for central-bank independence is primarily related to policy independence.

The best way to illustrate the argument is to present a "stripped" version of Rogoff's (1985) model. In Rogoff's model, society can sometimes improve its position by appointing a central banker who does not share the social-objective function but, instead, places a higher weight on price stability relative to output stabilization. In the simplified version, output is given by equation (1), in which the natural level of output is put at 0 and the parameters at 1. The timing of events in the Rogoff model is as follows: first, inflation expectations (π_t^e) are set (nominal-wage contracts are signed); then, the shock (u_t) occurs; and finally, the central banker sets the inflation rate (π_t). Society's loss function is given by

$$L_t = \frac{1}{2}\pi_t^2 + \frac{\chi}{2}(y_t - \hat{y}_t)^2 \,, \tag{6}$$

where the weight on output stabilization $\chi > 0$ and $\hat{y} > 0$, so that the desired level of output $(\hat{y})$ is above the natural level. Rogoff shows that it is optimal for society to choose an independent (conservative) central banker who assigns a higher weight to price stability in his loss function:

$$I_t = \frac{1+\varepsilon}{2}\pi_t^2 + \frac{\chi}{2}(y_t - \hat{y}_t)^2 \,, \tag{7}$$

where ε, the additional weight on the inflation goal, lies between zero and infinity $(0 < \varepsilon < \infty)$.

Substituting and taking first-order conditions with respect to π_t and solving for rational expectations, we obtain

$$\pi_t = \frac{\chi}{1 + \varepsilon}\hat{y} - \frac{\chi}{1 + \varepsilon + \chi}\mu_t \,. \tag{8}$$

Policy rule (8) shows that the introduction of a conservative central

---

[7] Waller (1992a) analyzes the appointment of a conservative central banker in a model that distinguishes between sectors that differ in their degree of competitiveness of the labor market. The main result of his paper is that, although agents in both sectors have the same preferences with respect to inflation and output stability, nominal-wage rigidity in the nonclassical labor market causes output in this sector to be more variable in equilibrium than in the classical sector. Consequently, if the classical sector were allowed to choose the "conservative" central banker, it would choose a more vigorous inflation fighter than the nonclassical sector would choose.

banker ($\varepsilon > 0$) leads to a lower inflationary bias and a lower variance of inflation. The variance of output is, however, an increasing function of the conservatism of the central banker. There is a trade-off between credibility and flexibility in the Rogoff model. It can be shown that the optimal value for ε, in terms of social-loss function (6), is positive but finite. This implies that it is optimal for society to appoint a conservative central banker.

Rogoff makes the crucial assumption that the central banker is completely independent and cannot be overridden *ex post* when the inflationary expectations (π_t^e) have been set and the policy is to be carried out. This may lead to large losses for society when extreme productivity shocks (u_t) occur. Lohmann (1992) introduces the possibility of overriding the central banker at a strictly positive but finite cost. Society's loss function therefore changes to

$$L_t' = \frac{1}{2}\pi_t^2 + \frac{\chi}{2}(y_t - \hat{y}_t)^2 + \delta c \, , \tag{9}$$

where δ is a dummy that takes on the value of 1 when the central bank is overridden and is 0 otherwise, and c is a cost that society incurs when the central bank is overridden. The central bank's loss function (7) stays the same.

The timing of events in the Lohmann model is as follows: In the first stage, the central banker's additional weight (ε) on the inflation goal is chosen, as is the cost (c) of overriding the central banker. The inflation expectations are then set. In the third stage, the productivity shock realizes, after which the central banker sets the inflation rate, which is either accepted or not. If it is not accepted, society overrides the central banker, incurs the cost (c), and resets the inflation rate. Finally, inflation and output realize.

In equilibrium, the central banker will not be overridden. In the case of an extreme productivity shock, he or she will set the inflation rate so that society will be indifferent between overriding or not. Rogoff's model is a special case of Lohmann's argument, where $c = \infty$. Lohmann shows that the optimal central-bank institution is characterized by $0 < \varepsilon^* < \infty$ and $0 < c^* < \infty$.

An important result from Rogoff's model is that the reduction in the equilibrium inflation rate that results from the appointment of a conservative and independent central banker generally comes at the expense of greater output variability from supply shocks, because the central banker offsets output shocks to a lesser extent than would the government.[8] Nevertheless, gains from lower inflation exceed losses from decreased stability. On net, therefore, society is made better off by appointing a conservative central banker. It is not optimal in the Rogoff model, however, to appoint a central banker whose only concern is low and stable inflation.

Rogoff's model has been criticized by McCallum (1995a), who contends that it is inappropriate simply to presume that the central bank behaves in a discretionary manner. It is more useful, he argues, to set the constant term and inflationary-expectations (π_t^e) coefficient in equation (3) equal to zero, thereby eliminating the inflationary bias while retaining the desirable countercyclical response to the shock (u_t). All that is needed to avoid the inflationary bias is for the central bank to recognize the futility of continually exploiting temporarily given expectations while planning not to do so in the future, and to recognize that the bank's objectives will be more fully achieved, on average, if it abstains from attempts to exploit these transient expectations. McCallum (1995b, p. 18) argues that "there is nothing tangible to prevent an actual central bank from behaving in this 'committed' or 'rule-like' fashion, so . . . some forward-looking banks will in fact do so. Analytical results that presume non-committed or discretionary behaviour may therefore be misleading." Although McCallum has a point, the problem is that a highly dependent central bank may not be able to behave in such a manner.

In addition to a legislative strategy, which will create, by law, an independent central bank and will mandate it, also by law, to direct its policies toward achieving price stability, other mechanisms have been suggested to overcome the incentive problems of monetary policy. The so-called contracting strategy regards the design of monetary institutions as one that involves structuring a contract between the central bank and the government. The optimal contract is an application of ideas from the literature on principal agents. In this application, the government is viewed as the principal, and the central bank is viewed as the agent. The principal signs a contract with the agent, according to which the bank is subject to an *ex post* penalty schedule that is linear in inflation. The nature of the contract will affect the incentives facing

[8] Recently, Alesina and Gatti (1995) have introduced another source of output variability in a model of the Rogoff type, namely, variability introduced in the system by the uncertainty about the future course of policy. This uncertainty results from uncertain electoral outcomes in the case in which there are two contending parties with different preferences regarding inflation and unemployment. In this circumstance, the overall effect of central-bank independence on output variability is ambiguous.

the bank and will, thereby, affect monetary policy (Walsh, 1993). Persson and Tabellini (1993) suggest a targeting strategy, in which the political principals of the central bank impose an explicit inflation target and make the central-bank leadership explicitly accountable for its success in meeting this target. Such a system has existed since 1989 in New Zealand, where the governor of the reserve bank may, under certain circumstances, be dismissed if the inflation rate exceeds 2 percent (see below for further details).

It is interesting to note that the analysis of Persson and Tabellini (1993) suggests that the optimal contract with a central bank implies no loss in terms of stabilization policy. As pointed out above, this result contrasts with the outcomes of most models in which monetary policy is delegated to an independent central bank, and credibility is increased at the expense of an optimal output-stabilization policy. Walsh (1993, 1995b) and Persson and Tabellini (1993) show that the optimal central-bank contract may serve to eliminate the inflation bias while still preserving the advantages of stabilization. This conclusion holds even if the central bank has private information.[9] It is thus clear that the contracting strategy is related to independence with respect to instruments but not with respect to goals.

The contracting strategy has also been criticized. For one thing, although the concept of social planners may be useful as a benchmark, these planners do not exist in practice. Hence, the government has to be relied on to impose the optimal incentive schedule on the central bank *ex post*. The government is also subject to an inflationary bias and usually to a greater extent than is the central bank (Cukierman, 1995). McCallum (1995a) argues that the optimal contract will not be credible if the government cannot commit to the optimal penalty schedule before various types of nominal contracts are concluded. A contract does not overcome the motivation for dynamic inconsistency; it merely relocates it.

Svensson (1995) has recently shown that when the objective function of the central banker differs from that of society with respect to the desired level of inflation (rather than the relative preference for price

[9] Walsh (1995b) also considers the situation in which candidates to head the central bank differ in their competency, the central bank's stance on monetary policy is not observable, and the informational content of a publicly observable signal about an aggregate supply shock is affected both by the central bank's competency and by the bank's implementation of given policies. In Walsh's model, the principal can induce the central bank to behave as demanded by using a contract that resembles an inflation-targeting rule with a reporting requirement.

stability), delegation of authority to a central banker with the "right" desired inflation level or target achieves the same results as the optimal contract. This implies that the socially optimal level of welfare can be achieved through delegation of authority to a central banker with a suitable desired level of inflation, rather than through an incentive contract for the bank. As pointed out by Cukierman (1995), the big advantage of the first institution is that it does not have to rely on the *ex post* implementation of the optimal contract by governments ridden by inflation bias. It would therefore appear that Svensson's result implies that it is possible to reach the social optimum simply by delegating authority to an appropriately chosen type of central banker. A practical difficulty that may prevent the implementation of such an institution is that the political principals may not be able to identify *ex ante* the levels of inflation potential candidates for central-bank leadership may desire. Svensson suggests that this problem may be circumvented by giving the bank independence only with regard to instruments, but not to goals, so that the target or "desired" rate of inflation in the bank's loss function is mandated by government.

Inflation Variability

The preceding analysis suggests that central-bank independence may reduce pre-election manipulation of monetary policy. If that is the case, central-bank independence may also result in more stable money growth and, therefore, less variability in inflation.

Another, related, argument also explains why central-bank independence may lead to less variability in inflation. Politicians not only strive to remain in office as long as possible, they are also partisan and wish to deliver benefits to their constituencies (Hibbs, 1977). Some evidence indicates that the pattern of unemployment and inflation is systematically related to the political orientation of governments. Whereas "right-wing" governments are generally thought to give a high priority to lower inflation, "left-wing" governments are often supposed to be more concerned about unemployment. Alesina (1988) reports that the unemployment rate in the United States is generally higher under Republican administrations than under Democratic administrations, whereas the inflation rate is lower under Republican administrations. Similar results have been reported by Havrilesky (1987) and Tabellini and La Via (1989). Existing evidence lends support to the view that the redistributional consequences of inflation provide an incentive for the political Left to endorse expansionary policies and for the Right to fight inflation (Alesina, 1989). This implies that inflation variability may be high if the government changes regularly, especially if the monetary authorities are dominated by elected politicians. A relatively independent central bank, however, will not change its policy after a new government has been elected. Central-bank autonomy may therefore reduce variability in inflation (Alesina, 1988).

Milton Friedman (1977) gives another reason why central-bank independence may affect inflation variability. Friedman wanted to explain why a positive correlation exists between the level of inflation and the variability of inflation across countries and over time for any given country. In Friedman's analysis, a government may temporarily pursue a set of policy goals (output, employment) that leads to high inflation; this, in turn, elicits strong political pressure to reduce the debasing of the currency. Chowdhury (1991) recently reexamined the relation between the level and the variability of inflation for a sample of sixty-six countries over the 1955–85 period. His results indicate the presence of a significant positive relation between the rate of inflation and its variability.

The Level and Variability of Economic Growth

Two opposing views have been expressed in the literature with respect to the effect of central-bank independence on the level of economic growth. Some authors have argued that the real interest rate depends on money growth; they assume that the Fisher hypothesis is nullified by the Mundell-Tobin effect.[10] A low level of inflation that is caused by a restrictive monetary policy results in high real interest rates, which may have detrimental effects on the level of investment and, hence, on economic growth (Alesina and Summers, 1993). There seems to be some evidence in support of the first part of the argument: countries with low levels of inflation have high *ex post* real interest rates (De Haan and Sturm, 1994a).

Other arguments, however, suggest that central-bank independence may further economic growth. As outlined above, an independent central bank may be less prone to political pressures and may therefore behave more predictably. This may enhance economic stability and reduce risk premia in interest rates, thereby stimulating economic growth (Alesina and Summers, 1993). In addition, central-bank independence

---

[10] A rise in expected inflation will lead, according to Mundell (1963), to the substitution of long-term financial assets for liquid assets and, according to Tobin (1965), to the substitution of physical-capital goods for liquid assets, thus lowering the marginal efficiency of capital and, thereby also, the expected (*ex ante*) real interest rates.

may moderate inflation. High levels of inflation may obstruct the price mechanism, and it is likely that this will hinder economic growth. Many economists, especially those involved in central banking, believe that even moderate rates of inflation impose significant economic costs on society (Fischer, 1993).[11] Recently, Grimes (1991) and Fischer (1993) have provided evidence to support the view that inflation harms economic growth.[12] One channel through which this effect may operate is increased inflation uncertainty. As noted above, a strong link exists between the level and the variability of inflation. Strong variation may lead to high inflation uncertainty, which, in turn, may damage economic growth. If central-bank independence reduces inflation variability and promotes less inflation uncertainty, the economy may prosper. Empirical studies on the links between inflation variability, inflation uncertainty, and economic growth, however, provide only mixed support for this point of view. Logue and Sweeney (1981), using annual data for twenty-four countries, find no evidence for a significant negative impact of inflation variability on real growth. A similar conclusion is reached by Jansen (1989). Engle (1983) finds little evidence for a link between inflation uncertainty and the relatively high rates of inflation experienced by the United States in the 1970s. Cukierman and Wachtel (1979), however, report a positive correlation between the rate of inflation and the dispersion of inflation forecasts gathered from the Michigan and Livingston inflation surveys. Evans (1991) has also published evidence consistent with the point of view that uncertainty about the long-term prospects for inflation is strongly linked to the actual rate of inflation.

Various theoretical positions have been delineated concerning the impact of central-bank independence on the *variability* of economic growth. One of these states that if the central bank introduces restrictive measures to combat inflation, it is likely to provoke recessions. In this view, inflation has become too high because the monetary authorities were too lax in previous periods. An independent central bank striving for price stability will not so easily let inflation run out of control and therefore will not follow such a stop-and-go policy. Fluctuations in real output will consequently be smaller (Alesina and Summers, 1993). Rogoff (1985), however, and Eijffinger and Schaling (1993b) conclude that when the central bank gives priority to price stability, the variability

[11] Fischer (1994) points out that the relation between inflation and economic growth may be nonlinear. Furthermore, the link between inflation and growth for low levels of inflation (1 to 3 percent) is difficult to determine empirically.

[12] See also Karras (1993), however, who argues that the correlation reported by Grimes (1991) is a consequence of the cyclical character of both variables.

of income will be greater than when the central bank also strives for stabilization of the economy.

It will have become clear by now that only empirical research can decide which view corresponds most closely to the data. Chapter 4 takes up this issue.

Objections to Central-Bank Independence

Various theoretical arguments have been given in support of central-bank autonomy. Chapter 4 will show that performance with regard to inflation is better, on average, in countries that have a relatively independent central bank than in countries in which the government more directly controls the central bank. Furthermore, various indications suggest that central-bank independence does not imply sacrifices in terms of lower output growth or higher unemployment.

Two objections have been raised against central-bank independence: the lack of democratic accountability and the potential damage to policy coordination (Goodhart, 1994). The final sections of this chapter will deal with these issues.

Accountability. The issue of the way in which central-bank independence relates to democratic accountability is discussed mainly in the Anglo-Saxon countries (Fischer, 1994; Eijffinger, 1994). Some authors have argued that monetary policy is just like other instruments of economic policy, such as fiscal policy, and so should be determined entirely by democratically elected representatives. Such a view implies, however, a too direct involvement of politicians with monetary policy. Nevertheless, in every democratic society, monetary policy has ultimately to be under the control of democratically elected politicians; one way or another, the central bank must be accountable. The parliament or, in the United States, the Congress, is responsible for central-bank legislation. In other words, the "rules of the game" (that is, the objectives of monetary policy) are settled by the legislatures in accordance with normal democratic procedures. The "game" (monetary policy), however, is delegated to the central banks. Because the parliament, or Congress, can alter legislation, the central bank remains under the ultimate control of the legislative body. Furthermore, in case the specified objective is not realized, the central bank, or the politician who bears final responsibility through his or her power to overrule the bank's policy, can be held accountable.

Central-bank independence and democratic accountability may be implemented in various ways. Each country organizes things differently. Three relatively independent central banks, the Deutsche Bundesbank,

15

the Nederlandsche Bank, and the Reserve Bank of New Zealand, exemplify the variations in approach. Five aspects of the division of responsibilities between the government and the central bank illustrate these differences (Roll et al., 1993):

(1) The ultimate objective(s) of monetary policy. The Reserve Bank of New Zealand has only one formal objective: price stability. Thus, the central bank is not independent with respect to its goals. The Bundesbank has a similar prime objective, which is, however, less specific—formally referred to as "defense of the value of the currency" (Casear, 1981; Kennedy, 1991). In addition, the Bundesbank has the obligation to offer general support to the government's economic policy in instances in which support does not prejudice the primary objective of price stability (Bundesbank Law 1957, section 12). This subsidiary statutory objective, however, is *de facto* unimportant. The objective of the Nederlandsche Bank is to regulate the value of the guilder in order to enhance welfare (Dutch Bank Law, section 9.1). This objective is nowadays interpreted as a stable exchange rate for the guilder vis-á-vis the deutsche mark.

(2) Precision of target specification. The Reserve Bank of New Zealand has to agree with the government on a tight target range for inflation for a three-year period. The Bundesbank has no obligation to agree to, obey, or announce any such targets. Since 1974, the Bundesbank has announced the targeted rate (or zone) for money growth, which implies an inflation target. The German government has been responsible for decisions about the exchange rate. This has been a reason for many conflicts between the Bundesbank and the government (Marsh, 1992).

(3) Statutory basis for independence. The Reserve Bank of New Zealand must agree with the government about a target for inflation but is free to choose its instruments (Debelle and Fischer, 1995). The Bundesbank is completely independent of any instruction from the government. It may consult the government, but it has no obligation to agree. Under section 13 of the Bundesbank Law 1957, government representatives have the right to attend meetings of the Zentralbankrat (Central Bank Council), but not to vote. The Dutch Bank Law of 1948 contains no specific articles on the statutory basis for the independence of the Nederlandsche Bank.

(4) Overriding the central bank. In New Zealand, the governor of the central bank can be dismissed if he fails to deliver the inflation target (*obligation ad hominem*). The contract ensures this by some clearly identified escape clauses, such as a rise in indirect taxes or a change in exchange-rate regime. In Germany, the government can suspend decisions of the Bundesbank for a maximum of two weeks (Bundesbank

16

Law 1957, section 13), a temporary veto that has seldom been formally deployed (Berger, 1995). Only through a change in the relevant legislation by a simple majority in parliament can the Bundesbank be overruled by the government. The Zentralbankrat is responsible for monetary policy (collective responsibility). The Netherlands has a unique central-bank legislation. According to section 26 of Dutch Bank Law, the minister of finance has the right to give an "instruction" to the bank with regard to monetary policy.[13] The right to give instructions makes the minister responsible for monetary policy vis-á-vis parliament.[14]

(5) Appointment of bank officials. In New Zealand, both the minister of finance and the board of the central bank must ratify the appointment of the governor (double veto). Board appointments are made by the finance minister, and the deputy governor is appointed by the board, on recommendation of the governor. In Germany, the Zentralbankrat is the governing board of the Bundesbank. Apart from the so-called Direktorium (Directorate), the presidents of the nine Landeszentralbanken (regional central banks) are members of the Zentralbankrat. The Direktorium is comprised of the president, the vice-president, and nowadays, a maximum of six other members, who are appointed by the president of the Federal Republic on nomination of the federal government.[15] The Zentralbankrat is consulted in this process. The presidents of the Landeszentralbanken are nominated by the Bundesrat (the upper federal chamber), based on recommendations from the governments of the Länder (states). The Zentralbankrat is then again consulted. In the Netherlands, the president and the director-secretary of the Nederlandsche Bank are appointed by the minister of finance, on the basis of a recommendation list containing only two names, which have been selected in a combined meeting of the governing board and the supervisory board of the bank (Dutch Bank Law, section 23). The other members of the governing board are also appointed by the minister, on

[13] This right is a kind of *ultimum remedium* and has never been applied. Zijlstra (1992), who was president of the Nederlandsche Bank between 1967 and 1981, recounts in his memoirs that Prime Minister Den Uyl (1974 to 1977) considered using this instrument after the bank had introduced credit restrictions in 1977.

[14] This construction is no longer allowed under the Maastricht Treaty. In the third phase of EMU, which according to the Treaty should start no later than 1999, the right of the minister of finance to give instructions to the central bank must be abolished.

[15] Before unification, each of the eleven western Länder had its own central bank; their presidents were members of the Zentralbankrat, as were the members of the Direktorium, which could maximally consist of ten persons, including the president and the vice-president of the Bundesbank. After unification, the number of Länder representatives was reduced to nine, and the maximum total for the Direktorium, to eight (Smith, 1994).

17

the basis of a recommendation list containing three names, again selected by the governing and supervisory boards. The royal commissioner is responsible for supervision on behalf of the government; he is also appointed by the minister (Dutch Bank Law, sections 30–31).

Table 1 summarizes the preceding analysis and indicates that central-bank independence in a democratic society may be implemented in different ways. According to the Maastricht Treaty, the ECB will become responsible for monetary policy within EMU. An important objection that has been raised to the ECB, however, is its lack of accountability (Gormley and De Haan, 1996). Indeed, the statutes of the ECB suggest that the democratic accountability of the ECB is poorly arranged, compared with the accountability of the central banks of the countries examined in this survey. This is true even in comparison with the Bundesbank, because the mandate of the ECB can only be changed through an amendment of the Treaty, which requires unanimity. By contrast, the Bundesbank must always take into account the possibility of a change of the law. Because of this, the Bundesbank will, in the long run, follow a policy that is in line with the preferences of democratically elected politicians. In the Netherlands, political approval is arranged differently, but the Nederlandsche Bank also pursues policies that generally enjoy broad political and popular support.

Coordination of Policies (This section draws heavily from Pollard, 1993). In addition to the lack of democratic accountability, potential problems in the coordination of economic policies have been put forward as an important argument against central-bank independence. Although most of the theoretical models discussed above make no clear distinction between monetary and fiscal policy, some theoretical studies concentrate on the conflicts that may arise when the government controls fiscal policy and the central bank controls monetary policy. Policymakers choose their own priorities concerning the goals for the economy, and the government and the central bank may cooperate or choose not to cooperate in implementing their policies. Andersen and Schneider (1986) distinguish three models of the economy that address this issue. In the first, Keynesian, model, even anticipated policy will affect the level of output and inflation. In the second, "Keynesian–New Classical" model, anticipated monetary policy is neutral; it can affect only inflation. In the third, "New Classical," model, anticipated monetary policy and fiscal policy can affect inflation but cannot affect output, and both the government and the central bank establish targets for inflation and output. Andersen and Schneider compare the economic outcomes under cooperation with those under noncooperation. Although

TABLE 1
ALTERNATIVE APPROACHES TO CENTRAL-BANK INDEPENDENCE
AND ACCOUNTABILITY

	Deutsche Bundesbank	Reserve Bank of New Zealand	Nederlandsche Bank
Policy objective			
Price stability	Primary objective	Sole objective	If welfare enhancing
Support of gov't economic policy	Secondary objective	—	—
Government override	Only implicit (new law)	Provision in current law	Right to give instruction
Policy targets			
Obligatory	No	Yes	No
As agreed with government	No	Yes	No
Escape clauses	No	Yes	No
Time horizon	No	Three years	No
Responsibility			
Vested in	Central-bank council	Governor of the central bank	Minister of finance
Monitoring	Only implicit	Dismissal of governor for failure	By royal commissioner

SOURCES: Roll et al., "Independent and Accountable" (1993), and the Dutch Central Bank Law of 1948.

the equilibrium level of output and the rate of inflation vary depending on the model used, the cooperative solution in all three models is Pareto superior to the noncooperative solution. This result is invariant, moreover, to the structure of noncooperation, be it Nash or Stackelberg. Andersen and Schneider (1986, p. 188) conclude that "two independent policymakers do not automatically guarantee a policy outcome which is preferred to other outcomes under different institutional solutions." Similar conclusions have been drawn by other authors (Hughes Hallett and Petit, 1990; Blake and Westaway, 1993).

Several comments are in order. First, many of these models take no account of a third "player," that is, trade unions or the general public.[16] As we have already seen, the perception the public has of the credibility

[16] This is not true for the model of Blake and Westaway (1993), which is similar to that of Barro and Gordon (1983). The conclusion these authors reach is that "it is unlikely to be sensible to appoint a monetary authority with an ability to make credible policy com-

of announced policies will affect macroeconomic outcomes. Second, most of these studies do not examine the sustainability of fiscal policy. As noted above, Sargent and Wallace (1981) have analyzed this issue, showing that if the government embarks on a path of unsustainable deficits, the central bank may eventually be forced to inflate to cover the deficit. If the public realizes that government debt is on such a path, it will expect inflation to increase, an expectation that may cause inflation to increase well before a debt limit is reached. Third, uncertainty about the macroeconomic models used by the policymakers may affect conclusions with respect to the usefulness of cooperation. Frankel and Rockett (1988) argue that, for the case in which the policymakers cooperate, model uncertainty may eventually yield negative outcomes. Fourth, many of the models referred to above equate central-bank independence with noncooperation between the fiscal and monetary authorities in policy implementation. This definition differs from the concept underlying the empirical indices for independence that are discussed in Chapter 3. As pointed out by Pollard (1993), differences in the definitions of independence may partly explain the diverging results of the theoretical models discussed above and the empirical studies that will be reviewed in Chapter 4.

Debelle (1993) deals with some of the shortcomings of this literature by differentiating between fiscal and monetary authorities in a model in which he also distinguishes private-sector agents (labor and firms).[17] He shows that, in addition to affecting central-bank independence, the objectives of the fiscal authorities also affect the inflation rate. Central-bank independence in this model, as in many others, is defined as the weight the central bank places on inflation relative to output (that is, how "conservative" the central bank is). Central-bank autonomy may reduce inflation, but it may also lead to lower social welfare, depending upon society's loss function.[18] In other words, the optimal degree of

---

mitments if at the same time it is following objectives which differ markedly from those of government itself" (Blake and Westaway, p. 79).

[17] The model draws on Alesina and Tabellini (1987). A similar model is presented by Debelle and Fischer (1995).

[18] Output is produced by labor, for which the nominal wage is predetermined; firms maximize profits and can hire the amount of labor they demand at the predetermined nominal wage. Social welfare is assumed to depend on inflation, the difference between the actual and the natural rate of production, and the difference between the target and actual level of government spending. The fiscal authorities have a similar loss function with different weights. Government spending is not included in the loss function of the monetary authorities. The simplest version of the model assumes that government

conservatism of the central bank depends on the society's aversion to inflation and output fluctuations.

---

spending can be financed only by seigniorage. It is clear why central-bank autonomy may result in lower social welfare, because a more independent central bank will yield not only lower inflation, but also a lower level of output and a lower level of government spending.

3   MEASURES OF CENTRAL-BANK INDEPENDENCE

It is difficult to measure the degree of legal independence central banks have, let alone the degree of their actual independence from government. Cukierman (1992) has pointed out that actual, as opposed to formal, independence hinges not only on legislation, but on a myriad of other factors as well, such as informal arrangements with the government, the quality of bank personnel, and the personal characteristics of key individuals at the bank. Because factors such as these are virtually impossible to quantify, most research has focused on legal independence; in addition, it is mainly restricted to the industrial countries. The three sections below discuss four widely used legal measures of central-bank independence, present a critical comparison of these indicators, and review some nonlegal indicators of central-bank independence.

Legal Measures of Central-Bank Independence

Table 2 presents four measures of central-bank independence, as developed by Alesina (1988, 1989), Grilli, Masciandaro, and Tabellini (1991), Eijffinger and Schaling (1992, 1993a), and Cukierman (1992), respectively. The higher the score is for the various indices, the more independent will be the central bank. The measures of Alesina and Eijffinger-Schaling range from 1 to 4, and 1 to 5, respectively. The index used by Grilli, Masciandaro, and Tabellini is the sum of their indicators for political and economic independence (see below for further details) and ranges from 3 to 13. The value for their index of political independence ranges from 0 to 6 and is shown in parentheses. The index of Cukierman varies from 0 to 1.

Although the indicators are all based on a similar approach, they sometimes show very different outcomes. According to the measure used by Grilli, Masciandaro, and Tabellini, for example, the Greek central bank has little autonomy; according to Cukierman's (1992) index, it is relatively independent. The remainder of this chapter briefly reviews these indicators; Appendix A provides more detailed information.

The pioneering attempt by Bade and Parkin (1988) to codify the legal independence of central banks has been extended by Alesina (1988, 1989). This index asks whether the central bank has final authority over monetary policy, whether government officials sit on the governing

TABLE 2

LEGAL INDICES OF CENTRAL-BANK INDEPENDENCE

Country	Alesina	Grilli, Masciandaro, and Tabellini	Eijffinger-Schaling	Cukierman (LVAU)
Australia	1	9 (3)	1	0.31
Austria	—	9 (3)	3[a]	0.58
Belgium	2	7 (1)	3	0.19
Canada	2	11 (4)	1	0.46
Denmark	2	8 (3)	4[a]	0.47
Finland	2	—	3[a]	0.27
France	2	7 (2)	2	0.28
Germany	4	13 (6)	5	0.66
Greece	—	4 (2)	—	0.51
Iceland	—	—	—	0.36
Ireland	—	7 (3)	—	0.39
Italy	1.5	5 (4)	2	0.22
Japan	3	6 (1)	3	0.16
Netherlands	2	10 (6)	4	0.42
New Zealand	1	3 (0)	3[a]	0.27
Norway	2	—	2[a]	0.14
Portugal	—	3 (1)	2[a]	—
Spain	1	5 (2)	3[a]	0.21
Sweden	2	—	2	0.27
Switzerland	4	12 (5)	5	0.68
United Kingdom	2	6 (1)	2	0.31
United States	3	12 (5)	3	0.51

NOTE: The Grilli, Masciandaro, and Tabellini measure is the sum of the indices for political and economic independence. Their index for political independence alone is shown in parentheses. LVAU is the unweighted legal-independence index.

[a] Extensions are based on Eijffinger and Van Keulen, "Central Bank Independence" (1995). Except for Denmark, the ranking of these seven countries refers to central-bank laws adjusted during the last ten years.

board of the bank, and whether more than half of the board members are appointed by the government.

Grilli, Masciandaro, and Tabellini (1991) present indices of political and economic independence. Their political-independence indicator focuses on appointment procedures for board members, the length of members' terms to office, and the existence of the statutory requirement to pursue monetary stability. Their economic-independence indicator considers the extent to which the central bank is free from government influence in implementing monetary policy. Generally, the total score for both political and economic independence is employed as an indicator for legal independence.

Eijffinger and Schaling (1992, 1993a) construct an index based on the location of final responsibility for monetary policy, the absence or presence of a government official on the board of the central bank, and the percentage of board appointees made by the government. Central-bank laws in which the central bank is the final authority get a double score.

Cukierman (1992) and Cukierman, Webb, and Neyapti (1992) provide an index that is aggregated from sixteen legal characteristics of central-bank charters grouped into four clusters: the appointment, dismissal, and legal term of office of the governor of the central bank; the institutional location of the final authority for monetary policy and the procedures for the resolution of conflicts between the government and the bank; the importance of price stability in comparison to other objectives; and the stringency and universality of limitations on the ability of the government to borrow from the central bank.

A Comparison of Legal-Independence Measures

Although all four measures are similar in principle, they yield quite different outcomes. This impression is confirmed by Table 3, which shows Kendall's rank-correlation coefficients of the various measures, with the Spearman rank correlation shown in parentheses. Note, especially, the low correlation of the measure of Grilli, Masciandaro, and Tabellini to the Cukierman and the Eijffinger-Schaling indices.

At least two explanations can be given for these diverging outcomes. First, the interpretation of the relevant bank laws differs. In general, one can say that different rankings will occur for those countries with which the author is most familiar. For instance, Alesina (1988, 1989) disagrees with the Bade–Parkin ranking for Italy. This does not lead to a higher ranking for the Banca d'Italia, however, but to a lower ranking. Eijffinger and Schaling (1992) conclude that Alesina (1988, 1989) implicitly includes a fourth criterion for Italy—namely, is the central bank obliged to accommodate the government budget deficit? Alesina does not, however, apply this criterion to the other countries in his sample.

In discussing the index of Grilli, Masciandaro, and Tabellini, Malinvaud (1991) argues that the Banque de France has been given a higher degree of independence than it actually merits, because the governor can be removed at any time by decision of the French government. In a similar vein, we have some doubts about Cukierman's (1992) interpretation of the Dutch central-bank law, with which we are most familiar. As explained in Appendix A, we believe that the Nederlandsche Bank is

TABLE 3

RANK-CORRELATION COEFFICIENTS OF INDICES OF CENTRAL-BANK INDEPENDENCE

	Alesina	Grilli, Masciandaro, and Tabellini	Eijffinger-Schaling	Cukierman (LVAU)
Alesina	1	0.58 (0.69)	0.71 (0.78)	0.38 (0.44)
Grilli, Masciandaro, and Tabellini	—	1	0.36 (0.48)	0.52 (0.63)
Eijffinger-Schaling	—	—	1	0.20 (0.35)
Cukierman (LVAU)	—	—	—	1

NOTE: Kendall rank-correlation coefficients are used, with Spearman rank-correlation coefficients in parentheses. The Grilli, Masciandaro, and Tabellini measure is the sum of the indices for political and economic independence. LVAU is the unweighted legal-independence index.

considerably more independent than Cukierman's coding suggests.[19]

A second reason for the diverging outcomes of various indicators is that the measures focus on different aspects of central-bank independence. Eijffinger and Schaling (1993a) criticize as "watered down" the measure Grilli, Masciandaro, and Tabellini (1991) use, because the rather large number of criteria that these authors apply erodes the weight of the most important criteria, which are the central-bank objectives and the appointing procedures. Cukierman's indicator may also be criticized in this respect. His aggregation procedures suggest that the criteria we believe to be the most important in determining central-bank autonomy (the variables in clusters 1 and 3) receive a relatively low weight.

More generally, these indices may be compared to the four aspects of central-bank independence outlined in Chapter 1. Table 4 shows how the four previous indicators plus that of Bade and Parkin (1988) focus on different aspects of central-bank independence. Because the measures differ and show a low correlation, it is doubtful that a reliable indicator for central-bank independence can be constructed from an average of various independence measures—as, for instance, Alesina and Summers (1993) and Fratianni and Huang (1994) have done.

[19] The Dutch Bank Law is apparently difficult to interpret. Roll et al. (1993, p. 27) are clearly wrong when they state that there is a "17-member Council that advises [the finance] minister of guidelines that [the] Bank should follow in policy."

TABLE 4

ASPECTS OF CENTRAL-BANK INDEPENDENCE: A COMPARISON OF FIVE INDICATORS

Measure	Bade-Parkin	Alesina	Grilli, Masciandaro, and Tabellini	Eijffinger-Schaling	Cukiermans (LVAU)
Maximum total score	4.00	4.00	16.00	5.00	1.00
Personnel independence	2.67	2.00	6.00	2.50	0.20
Financial independence	—	1.00	5.00	—	0.50
Policy independence	1.33	1.00	5.00	2.50	0.30
Goal independence	—	—	2.00	—	0.15
Instrument independence	—	—	3.00	—	0.15

Nonlegal Measures of Central-Bank Independence

Cukierman (1992) develops a measure for central-bank independence on the basis of answers to a questionnaire under "qualified individuals in various central banks." He gives both an unweighted (QVAU) and a weighted (QVAW) variant of this indicator. The questionnaire examined five issues: (1) legal aspects of independence; (2) actual practice when it differs from the stipulation of the law; (3) monetary-policy instruments and the agencies controlling them; (4) intermediate targets and indicators, and (5) final objectives of monetary policy and their relative importance. Unfortunately, the responding number of central bankers was rather limited. Furthermore, an obvious methodological drawback of the questionnaire is that central bankers may benefit from providing a too positive impression of their independence. It is therefore doubtful that the personnel of central banks are the most appropriate recipients for a questionnaire on central-bank autonomy.[20] To the best of our knowledge, however, a similar survey has never been organized among other financial-market participants.

Cukierman (1992) and Cukierman, Webb, and Neyapti (1992) have also developed a yardstick for central-bank autonomy based on the actual average term of office of central-bank governors in a number of countries from 1950 to 1989. This indicator is based on the presumption that a higher turnover of central-bank governors indicates a lower level of independence, at least above some threshold, and that even if

[20] Indeed, one can argue that the difference between the legal-independence measure and the indicator based on the questionnaire gives some impression of the degree to which central bankers overrate their independence. For example, the score for Cukierman's unweighted legal-independence index (LVAU) for Italy is 0.22, whereas the score for QVAU is 0.76.

the central-bank law is quite explicit, it may not be operational if a different tradition has precedence. A striking example is Argentina, where the legal term of office of the central-bank governor is four years, but where there is also an informal tradition that the governor will resign whenever there is a change of government, or even a new finance minister. Consequently, the actual average term of office of Argentinean central-bank governors during the 1980s amounted to only ten months. This example suggests that the turnover rate of central-bank governors may be a good indicator for the degree of central-bank autonomy.[21] Table 5 presents the average turnover rate of central-bank governors for fifty-five industrial and developing countries during the forty years ending in 1989. Two conclusions may be drawn from the table. First, the turnover rate differs greatly across countries, varying from 0.03, for Iceland, to 0.93, for Argentina. Second, the average and standard deviations of the turnover rate for developing countries are much higher than the corresponding measures for industrial countries. The average turnover rate for the developing countries is 0.28; the average for the industrial countries is 0.13. The highest turnover rate in the industrial countries (excluding Turkey) is 0.2, for Spain and Japan. This measure of autonomy therefore hardly discriminates between the central banks of the industrial countries.

Cukierman and Webb (1995) have gone one step further. They argue that the frequency of transfers of central-bank governors reflects both the frequency of political change (shifts in regime, for example, or in the head of government) and the percentage of political changes that are followed by changes in the governorship of the central bank. They therefore develop an indicator of the *political vulnerability* of the central bank, which is defined as the percentage of political transitions that are followed within 6 months by the replacement of the central-bank governor. For the period from 1950 to 1989, they calculate that the average index of political vulnerability is 0.24 (0.10 for industrial countries; 0.34 for developing countries). Again, one should be careful in interpreting this index. De Haan (1995a) shows that the score of 0.10 for the Netherlands is the result of pure coincidence.

It follows from the foregoing analysis that existing indices of central-bank independence are often incomplete and noisy indicators of actual

---

[21] A long term in office may also indicate a low level of independence, because a relatively subservient governor will tend to stay longer in office than will a governor who stands up to the executive branch. Cukierman (1992) argues that this may be true for countries with exceptionally low turnover rates, such as Denmark, Iceland, and the United Kingdom.

TABLE 5

THE TURNOVER RATE OF CENTRAL-BANK GOVERNORS, 1950–1989

Industrial Countries		Developing Countries		Developing Countries (*contd.*)	
Belgium	0.13	Argentina	0.93	Philippines	0.13
Canada	0.10	Bahamas	0.19	Singapore	0.37
Denmark	0.05	Barbados	0.11	South Africa	0.10
Finland	0.13	Botswana	0.41	South Korea	0.43
France	0.15	Chili	0.45	Tanzania	0.13
Germany	0.10	Colombia	0.20	Thailand	0.20
Greece	0.18	Costa Rica	0.58	Uganda	0.34
Iceland	0.03	Egypt	0.31	Uruguay	0.38
Ireland	0.15	Ethiopia	0.20	Venezuela	0.30
Italy	0.08	Ghana	0.28	Zaire	0.23
Japan	0.20	Honduras	0.13	Zambia	0.38
Luxembourg	0.08	India	0.33	Zimbabwe	0.15
Netherlands	0.05	Israel	0.14		
New Zealand	0.15	Kenya	0.17		
Norway	0.08	Lebanon	0.19		
Spain	0.20	Malaysia	0.13		
Sweden	0.15	Malta	0.28		
Switzerland	0.13	Mexico	0.15		
Turkey	0.40	Nigeria	0.19		
United Kingdom	0.10	Panama	0.24		
United States	0.13	Peru	0.33		
Average	0.13	Average			0.28
Standard deviation	0.08	Standard deviation			0.17

SOURCE: Cukierman, *Central Bank Strategy* (1992). The (previously) Communist countries are not included.

independence. This does not mean that they are uninformative, but it does imply, as pointed out by Cukierman (1995), that their use should be supplemented by judgment of the problem under consideration. In particular, certain indices are more appropriate for some purposes than for others. Measures of legal independence, for example, may be a better proxy for independence in industrial countries than in developing countries. In some cases, various proxies that capture different aspects of central-bank independence may be usefully combined to get a more complete picture. Legal measures of central-bank independence are more likely to be exogenous with respect to the economy, but because they vary little over time, they are generally poor explainers of developments in economic variables within countries. Most empirical studies on the consequences of central-bank independence are therefore cross-sectional.

4 EMPIRICAL EVIDENCE ON THE CONSEQUENCES OF CENTRAL-BANK INDEPENDENCE

This chapter examines the empirical evidence for a link between central-bank independence and various economic variables such as inflation and economic growth. Appendix B summarizes all the studies of which we are aware that use one or more of the independence indicators discussed in Chapter 3. One conclusion that follows from this summary is that most of the studies are confined to the industrial countries. Another insight is that many authors consider only one measure of central-bank independence, so that the conclusions they draw may be "measure specific." Because the independence indicators used focus on different aspects of central-bank independence, it is important to use various indicators, even if the sample includes only industrial countries. Some studies compare the findings when several indicators are used, thereby examining the robustness of the empirical results. As will be shown below, some outcomes do, indeed, depend on which indicator is used for central-bank independence.

The Level and Variability of Inflation

The well-known inverse relation between central-bank independence and the level of inflation is supported by most empirical studies (see Table B2 for a summary of the conclusions reached). An exception is Cargill (1995), who argues that this statistical association is not robust and depends on the countries and periods included and on the regression specification. His argument is unconvincing, however, because he uses only one measure of central-bank independence—and also because he presents the outcomes of various model specifications without analyzing which specification is to be preferred from an econometric perspective. Furthermore, one would expect different results under fixed and under floating exchange-rate regimes (see also Cukierman, Rodriguez, and Webb, 1995). Under the Bretton Woods system of fixed exchange rates, countries were committed to an exchange-rate target and had little room to conduct an autonomous domestic monetary policy. Thus, the relation between central-bank independence and inflation is likely to be much less straightforward for the period before 1973. Regression analyses by Grilli, Masciandaro, and Tabellini (1991) and De Haan and Sturm (1994a) support this view.[22] Indeed, one can argue that if no evidence of a relation between independence and inflation is found in the Bretton Woods period, although such a link is found for the post–Bretton Woods era, the argument that central-bank independence is a primary determinant of a country's inflation performance will be strengthened (Pollard, 1993). Still, many authors lack precision in distinguishing between exchange-rate regimes.

Despite the overwhelming evidence in support of a negative relation between central-bank independence and inflation, it should be noted that a negative correlation does not necessarily imply causation. The correlation between the variables can perhaps be explained by a third factor (for example, the culture and tradition of monetary stability in a country) that explains both an independent central bank and low inflation.[23] Similarly, there may be a two-way causality between inflation and central-bank independence. It is likely that less independence contributes to higher inflation. But high inflation may also affect independence. As will be explained in more detail in Chapter 5, it can be argued that high inflation leads to more or to less central-bank independence. On the one hand, high inflation may lead to political pressure for low inflation; on the other, it may encourage processes that make it easier for the government to influence monetary policy, thereby reducing actual independence. Most studies do not address this issue of two-way causality. Cukierman (1992) and Cukierman, Webb, and Neyapti (1992) deal with this issue by using two-stage least-squares and instrumental variables. They conclude that there is a vicious circle between inflation and low levels of independence. When sufficiently sustained, inflation erodes central-bank independence. Then, low independence contributes to higher inflation. De Haan and Van 't Hag (1995) conclude, however, that high levels of inflation in the past led eventually to more central-bank independence.

[22] Similarly, one would expect that the Exchange Rate Mechanism (ERM) of the EMS might affect outcomes. Ungerer (1990) characterizes the first phase of the EMS (1979 to 1982) as a period of "initial orientation" full of frequent and, sometimes, large realignments of central rates. From 1982 onward, however, the EMS entered a second phase of "consolidation" (1982 to 1987), and after the accord of Basle-Nyborg, it moved into a third phase of "reexamination" (1987 to the present). The negative correlation between central-bank independence and inflation is thus expected to be less clear-cut during the second and third subperiods than during the first, because the priority EMS countries initially gave to exchange-rate stability was not given subsequently. Regression analyses by Eijffinger and Schaling (1993b) and De Haan and Eijffinger (1994) support this view.

[23] The standard example is the case of Germany, where the hyperinflation in the 1920s led to a culture and tradition of monetary stability (Bresciani–Turroni, 1953).

There is evidence that inflation and political instability are positively associated. Some recent studies show that even if some measure of political instability is included in the regression, proxies for central-bank independence, such as the turnover rate of central-bank governors or the political vulnerability of the central bank, remain significantly related to inflation (De Haan and Siermann, 1994; Cukierman and Webb, 1995).

As mentioned, most of the studies summarized in Appendix B are confined to industrial countries, although developing countries are included in the studies of Cukierman (1992), Cukierman, Webb, and Neyapti (1992), Cukierman et al. (1993), De Haan and Siermann (1994), and Cukierman and Webb (1995). For the developing countries considered, these authors find no significant link between inflation and the legal independence of the central banks. They believe that this is because the developing countries have "less regard for the law"; industrial countries, by contrast, exhibit an inverse relation between the legal-independence measure and inflation. If the turnover rate of central-bank governors is used as a measure of actual independence in the developing countries, however, a significant, negative relationship appears for the developing countries as well.[24] Similar results are found by Cukierman and Webb (1995), using the political vulnerability of the central bank as an indicator for central-bank independence.

Most empirical studies consist of simple cross-sectional estimates in which the average inflation rate is "explained" by some measure of central-bank independence. Some authors, however, include additional explanatory variables. Grilli, Masciandaro, and Tabellini (1991) and De Haan and Sturm (1994a), for example, include some indicators for political instability. This does not rob the coefficients of the independence indicators of their significance. Similarly, Havrilesky and Granato (1993) and Bleaney (1996) take wage-bargaining structures into account, and Al-Marhubi and Willett (1995), employ indicators for openness, degree of exchange-rate fixity, and budget deficits. Once again, the coefficients of the various indicators for central-bank independence remain significant.

Although many empirical studies examine the relation between central-bank independence and inflation, only two studies try to differentiate between the various aspects of central-bank autonomy. Debelle and Fischer (1995) decompose the independence measure of Grilli,

---

[24] Although there are only twenty-two observations available for the 1980s, the independence index based on the questionnaire with central bankers also has the predicted sign and is statistically very significant.

31

Masciandaro, and Tabellini (1991) into independence with respect to goals, personnel, and instruments.[25] They conclude that lack of goal independence (that is, a mandate to maintain price stability) and instrument independence are most closely tied to inflation performance, whereas personnel independence is not significantly related to inflation. Similarly, De Haan (1995b) has decomposed the legal-independence measure of Cukierman (1992) and relates its components to inflation. Using pooled time-series and cross-sectional data for a sample of twenty-one industrial countries, he concludes that only independence with respect to instruments matters for inflation performance.[26] Table 6 reproduces some results from these studies.

As explained above, most empirical studies on the relation between central-bank independence and inflation consist of cross-sectional regressions. Other studies, however, follow a somewhat different approach. Capie, Mills, and Wood (1994) investigate the relation between the level of inflation and central-bank independence for twelve countries: Austria(-Hungary), Belgium, Brazil, Canada, England (the United Kingdom), France, (West-) Germany, India, Italy, Japan, New Zealand, Spain, Sweden, and the United States. Based on the degree of policy influence, beginning between 1871 and 1916 and ending in 1987, central banks in these countries are classified as "independent," "dependent," or "unclassified." During all periods—before World War I, during the interwar period, and during and after the Bretton Woods system— the nations with independent central banks have continuously been in the group of countries with low inflation. Sometimes this group has also included countries with dependent central banks. Capie, Mills, and Wood conclude, therefore, that independence is a sufficient, but not a necessary, condition for low inflation.

---

[25] Goal independence is measured as the presence of a statutory requirement that the central bank pursue monetary stability among its goals. Personnel independence is measured as the Grilli–Masciandaro–Tabellini index of political independence, excluding the statutory requirement. Instrument independence is the Grilli–Masciandaro–Tabellini index of economic independence minus the bank-supervision criterion.

[26] The proxy for personnel independence is the sum of all variables in the first cluster of variables distinguished by Cukierman (1992)—and explained in some detail in Chapter 3. The proxy for instrument independence is the sum of the variables in the second cluster, except for whether the central bank has an active role in the formulation of the government's budget, which has little to do with central-bank independence. Goal independence is Cukierman's (1992) score for the third cluster; according to Cukierman (1992, p. 377), "it proxies the . . . independence of the CB to elevate the target of price stability above other objectives. In Rogoff's terminology, it measures how strong is the 'conservative bias' of the CB as embodied in the law." Financial independence is proxied by the sum of most variables in the fourth cluster, as discerned by Cukierman (1992).

TABLE 6

REGRESSIONS OF INFLATION ON ASPECTS OF CENTRAL-BANK INDEPENDENCE

Study	Goal Independence	Instrument Independence	Personnel Independence	Financial Independence
Debelle and Fischer (1995)	-1.76 (1.02)	-1.02 (2.04)[a]	-0.41 (0.91)	—
	-2.28 (1.42)	-1.02 (2.04)[a]	—	—
De Haan (1995b)	2.33 (1.12)	-2.27 (-2.01)[a]	-0.16 (-0.26)	-0.58 (-0.95)
	2.13 (1.10)	-3.02 (-3.83)[b]	-0.36 (-0.58)	—

NOTE: t-statistics are in parentheses.
[a] Denotes significance at the 5 percent level.
[b] Denotes significance at the 1 percent level.

Johnson and Siklos (1994) use reaction functions of central banks, with the money-market interest rate as the policy variable. If central-bank independence can be measured by the change in interest rates, little difference can be discerned across the central banks considered. The analysis of Johnson and Siklos covers seventeen industrial countries from 1960 to 1990.

Eijffinger, Van Rooij, and Schaling (1994) apply a panel-data approach to the reaction functions of the central banks of ten industrial countries for the 1977–90 period, using present and past inflation and real economic growth as the explanatory variables of changes in money-market rates. They find a country-specific factor that they interpret as the degree of empirical central-bank independence. Regression analysis of average inflation on their empirical index (EMP) of central-bank independence confirms that having an independent central bank will lead to lower inflation.

The main conclusion from empirical studies on the relation between central-bank autonomy and inflation is that central-bank independence is inversely related to the level of inflation in both the industrial and the developing countries. The independence measures used to reach this conclusion, however, differ between the two groups of countries. Although legal independence is a good proxy for actual autonomy in industrial countries, proxies such as the turnover rate of the central-bank governorship or the political vulnerability of the central bank should be used for developing countries.

What is the empirical relation between central-bank independence and the variability of inflation? Inflation variability is positively correlated with the level of inflation (Chowdhury, 1991). Consequently, if a high degree of central-bank independence results in lower levels of inflation, greater independence may also lead to less variability of inflation. Indeed, as shown in Appendix B, many authors conclude that the variability of inflation—generally measured as the standard deviation of inflation—shows an inverse relation to central-bank independence. This concurs with Rogoff's (1985) model.

There is another way to consider the impact of central-bank independence on the variability of inflation. As shown in Chapter 2, partisan considerations will lead to inflation variability if the government changes regularly and if the monetary authorities are dominated by elected politicians. In contrast, a relatively independent central bank will not change its policy after a new government has been elected. Central-bank independence may therefore reduce inflation variability over longer periods of time. Table 7 updates and extends a table provided by Alesina (1988), in which he analyzes differences in the influence central-bank independence has on inflation under "right-wing" and "left-wing" governments. Only those countries that during the 1980s witnessed a change in government in which a right-wing government replaced a left-wing government, or vice versa, and in which a meaningful comparison is possible, are included in Table 7. The first three rows give an update of the data provided by Alesina (1988), who concludes that inflation shows little variation between governments with different political orientations in countries with relatively independent central banks. The lower part of the table presents our extension to Australia, New Zealand, and Norway. It follows that Alesina's conclusion depends strongly on the specific countries included in the analysis. When Australia, New Zealand, and Norway are also included, the results are less clear-cut. First, the inflation rate is lower under "left-wing" governments in these three countries than under "right-wing" governments. Second, the inflation differentials seem hardly to be related to central-bank independence. Norway, for instance, has a relatively dependent central bank, according to the index Cukierman (1992) uses, but its inflation differentials are similar to those of Australia and New Zealand.

Economic Growth and Disinflation Costs

The foregoing analysis put forward two reasons why central-bank independence may stimulate economic growth in the long run: less

34

TABLE 7

AVERAGE INFLATION IN SIX INDUSTRIAL COUNTRIES UNDER "LEFT-WING" AND "RIGHT-WING" GOVERNMENTS

Country	Government, Period, and Percent Inflation		Percent Difference between Governments	Measures of Central-Bank Independence	
				GMT	LVAU
Australia	Frazer (Liberal) (1976–83): 10.3	Hawk (Labor) (1984–90): 7.2	3.1	9	0.31
Germany	Social Democrats (1975–82): 4.8	Christian Democrats (1983–92): 2.4	2.4	13	0.66
New Zealand	Muldoon (National Party) (1976–84): 13.6	Lange/Palmer/Moore (Labor) (1985–90): 10.5	3.1	9	0.27
Norway	Willoch (Conservative) (1982–86): 7.9	Brundlandt (Social Democrat) (1987–92): 4.9	3.0	—	0.14
United Kingdom	Labor (1975–79): 15.4	Conservatives (1980–92): 6.8	8.6	6	0.31
United States	Carter (Democrat) (1977–80): 8.4	Reagan (Republican) (1981–92): 4.7	3.7	12	0.51

NOTE: GMT = Grilli, Masciandaro, and Tabellini. LVAU = Cukierman's unweighted legal-independence index; the higher the score, the more independent the central bank is.

uncertainty about inflation and better functioning of the price mechanism. Empirical research by Grimes (1991), Fischer (1993), and Barro (1995) suggests that inflation reduces economic growth.[27] This may be explained by the positive correlation between the level and variability of inflation. Greater variation in the rate of inflation may imply increasing uncertainty about inflation and may thereby lead to lower economic growth. This relation between inflation variability and economic growth, however, is not supported by most studies. Logue and Sweeney (1981) find no significant influence of inflation variability on real growth rates. Jansen (1989) draws the same conclusion.

Various studies have asked directly whether central-bank independence is related to economic growth. A summary of these studies (Appendix B) shows that various authors conclude that central-bank independence is not related to economic growth (or to unemployment). Despite the association of a high degree of central-bank independence with lower inflation in the long run, a policy of disinflation is apparently not associated with high costs or great benefits in terms of long-term economic growth. Indeed, it is tempting to conclude that the absence of a long-term trade-off between inflation and growth implies that the establishment of central-bank independence is a free lunch. Recall, however, that price stability is generally regarded as an essential condition for sustainable economic growth and that central-bank independence should accordingly lead to a higher level of economic growth. From this point of view, lack of a significant, positive relation between growth and independence would be disappointing. Two studies exist, however, that report a positive relation between central-bank autonomy and economic growth. De Long and Summers (1992) find a positive relation between central-bank independence and gross domestic product (GDP) per worker for their sample of industrial countries. Cukierman et al. (1993) find that economic growth is not correlated with central-bank independence in the industrial countries, even after corrections are made for other factors that may influence growth. They find that it is positively correlated with growth in the developing countries, however, if the frequency of changes of central-bank presidents is used as a proxy for independence.

A next question, of course, is whether a relationship exists between central-bank independence and the variation of economic growth. Alesina and Summers (1993) argue that an autonomous central bank will be less inclined to conduct a stop-and-go policy, which may limit

[27] A recent study by Karras (1993), however, contradicts this conclusion.

fluctuations in economic growth. Most researchers find that a higher degree of central-bank independence is generally not associated with greater variation of real economic growth rates (see Appendix B).

The greater credibility attributed to independent central banks is often thought to reduce the costs of subsequent policies designed to cut inflation. Increased central-bank independence tends to shift the short-term Phillips curve inward to the origin. Walsh (1995a) has pointed out, however, that central-bank independence may also affect the slope of the Phillips curve. If, for instance, independent central banks foster an economic environment that produces nominal-wage contracts of longer duration or with less indexation because inflation is less variable, nominal rigidities in the economy will increase, thereby flattening the slope of the Phillips curve. The effect on the slope of the short-term trade-off between unemployment and inflation will raise the real economic costs of a policy to diminish inflation. This can, in turn, reduce, and potentially offset, the reduced costs of disinflation attributed to the gain in credibility that comes with increased independence.

Another reason why there may be a positive relation between central-bank independence and the costs of disinflation has been put forward by Gärtner (1995). In order to keep disinflation costs at a minimum in a framework of staggered wage contracts and relative-wage considerations, disinflation must start slowly and accelerate only as the bulk of wage contracts has been renegotiated (see also Taylor, 1983). Because more independent central banks are likely to disinflate faster, they will face higher disinflation costs.

The net effect of independence on the costs of disinflation is an empirical question. De Haan, Knot, and Sturm (1993) ask whether central-bank independence reduces disinflation costs (measured as the cumulated unemployment rate over the 1980–89 period relative to its average level for 1973–79); they find no supporting evidence that it does. Four more recent studies also analyze the effects of central-bank independence on the costs of disinflation. Debelle and Fischer (1995) compare the output costs of recessions in Germany and the United States and find that the costs are similar. The sacrifice ratio (output lost because of the inflation reduction) in Germany is larger than in the United States for all recent recessions, despite the widely assumed "credibility bonus" of the Bundesbank. Debelle and Fischer also report a positive and significant relation between the Grilli-Masciandaro-Tabellini index of central-bank independence and output losses. Similar results are reported by Gärtner (1995) and Andreas Fischer (1996),

37

who use other indicators as well for central-bank independence.[28] Posen (1994) also concludes that the costs of disinflation are not lower in countries with independent central banks, even when differences in contracting behavior are taken into account. All this evidence implies that output losses suffered during recessions have, on average, been larger as the independence of the central bank increases. As Debelle and Fischer argue, this suggests that no credibility bonus exists in the labor markets for more independent central banks: the banks have to prove their toughness by continually being tough. Similar results have been reported by Walsh (1995a) for various EU member states. European Union countries with greater central-bank independence also appear to face higher costs of disinflation. Walsh has pointed out that this positive correlation could arise because inflation is more costly to reduce at lower levels of inflation, and central-bank independence is associated with lower levels of inflation. Walsh also reports evidence, however, that even after controlling for average inflation in a cross-sectional regression of EU countries, the relation between the trade-off parameter and central-bank independence is positive and significant. According to Walsh, this evidence suggests that the greater central-bank independence required under the Maastricht Treaty may lead to a rise within EMU of the costs associated with policies designed to reduce inflation. Still, one should bear in mind that the causality may run in the other direction. Perhaps countries with flat short-term aggregate supply curves will be more likely to establish independent central banks. Walsh has noticed that flat supply curves make disinflation more costly, but they also raise the temptation to stimulate the economy and thus increase the inflationary bias of discretionary policy. This issue will be taken up in Chapter 5.

Other Variables

It follows from the preceding analysis that greater central-bank inde-pendence is associated with lower inflation rates. Through the Mundell-Tobin effect, this may result in higher (*ex post*) real interest rates. De Haan and Sturm (1994a) find some limited support for the Mundell-Tobin effect: low inflation countries usually have high (*ex post*) real interest rates. It can also be argued, however, that more independence dampens inflation uncertainty and, through the Mascaro–Meltzer (1983)

---

[28] Gärtner's results differ from Taylor's (1983), however, because they show no relation between central-bank independence and the speed of disinflation. Fischer reports that independent central banks deflate more slowly.

effect, brings down (*ex post*) real interest rates.[29] These opposite effects on the real interest rate might also explain why the net effect on economic growth turns out to be insignificant. Alesina and Summers (1993) examine the link between central-bank independence and the (*ex post*) real interest rate and find no clear relationship. Nevertheless, these authors discover a negative correlation between central-bank independence and the variability of (*ex post*) real interest rates.

Is there, finally, some relation between central-bank independence and (the monetary accommodation of) government budget deficits? One would expect that an independent central bank is in a better position to resist the pressure of its government to accommodate budget deficits by means of monetary financing. Moreover, the government has a strong incentive, when budget deficits are financed on the capital market, to reduce the deficit so as to minimize future interest payments.

Parkin (1987) concludes that Germany and Switzerland, the two countries in his sample with the most independent central banks, appear to have almost no government deficits in the period under consideration. Masciandaro and Tabellini (1988) rate Australia, Canada, Japan, New Zealand, and the United States, taking the budget deficit as a ratio of gross national product (GNP) for the period from 1970 to 1985. They find that New Zealand, with (until recently) the least independent central bank, has the highest average deficit over this period, whereas the United States, with (according to Masciandaro and Tabellini) the most independent central bank, has a deficit equal to that of the remaining three countries.

Grilli, Masciandaro, and Tabellini (1991) also find for their measure a negative correlation between the deficit and the degree of independence from 1950 to 1989, although it is not significant. Their results are supported by De Haan and Sturm (1994a).[30] Pollard (1993) finds a negative correlation between central-bank independence and the deficit-to-GDP ratio that also appears not to be significant. Quite strangely, however, Pollard discovers a significant, negative relation between independence and the *variance* of the budget deficit as a percentage of GDP.

[29] According to Mascaro and Meltzer (1983), monetary and inflationary uncertainty, measured by the variability of (unexpected) money growth and inflation, respectively, will result in a risk premium that risk-averse investors will demand in order to compensate for uncertainty and, thereby, in a higher (*ex ante*) real interest rate (see also Bomhoff, 1983).

[30] Note that in case of the Grilli-Masciandaro-Tabellini index, there is the danger of circular reasoning because their (modified) index comprises at least four elements of monetary accommodation of government deficits. The empirical evidence found by Grilli, Masciandaro, and Tabellini and De Haan and Sturm is therefore not at all surprising.

Our prudent conclusion is that an independent central bank cannot restrain its government from creating budget deficits, but that it may have some restrictive influence on the fiscal policies pursued by its government.

What should we make of the preceding review of empirical studies on the relation between central-bank independence and macroeconomic variables such as inflation and growth? Is it true, as Grilli, Masciandaro, and Tabellini (1991, p. 375) claim, that "having an independent bank is almost like having a free lunch; there are benefits but no apparent costs in terms of macroeconomic performance"? Although overwhelming evidence exists that central-bank independence and inflation are negatively related, one should be careful in jumping to this conclusion. As has been pointed out, only limited support exists for the view that central-bank independence stimulates economic growth and that it does not reduce disinflation costs. Furthermore, central-bank independence may be endogenous, in the sense that countries with a commitment to price stability may have a greater propensity for central-bank independence. If true, the mere establishment of a central bank with a commitment to price stability will not bring inflation benefits to a country. The following chapter analyzes the determinants of central-bank independence.

5 THE DETERMINANTS OF CENTRAL-BANK INDEPENDENCE

The previous chapters have shown that the degree of central-bank independence varies considerably among the industrial countries. The question is which factors ultimately determine the degree of central-bank independence. It is remarkable that a literature dealing with this issue has hardly developed. Before discussing some of the determinants of central-bank independence in greater detail, we shall first review recently developed theory.

Cukierman (1994) presumes that the delegation of monetary policy to (partly) independent central banks is used as a "(partial) commitment device." By specifying the objectives of the central bank more or less tightly and by giving the bank broader or narrower powers, politicians determine the extent of their commitment to a policy rule. Such policy action leads to greater credibility of monetary policy, which, in turn, is reflected in lower inflationary expectations and, thereby, lower (capital-market) interest rates and more moderate wage demands. From the politician's point of view, the costs of an independent central bank consist mainly of the loss of flexibility in monetary policymaking. The balance between flexibility and credibility determines the optimal degree of central-bank autonomy in a country. Based on these or other theoretical considerations, various economic and political determinants of central-bank independence have been formulated. These determinants may be categorized as follows (note that they are not mutually exclusive and may partly overlap). They are (1) the equilibrium or natural rate of unemployment; (2) the stock of government debt; (3) political instability; (4) the supervision of financial institutions; (5) financial opposition to inflation; (6) public opposition to inflation; and (7) other determinants.

Table 8 summarizes empirical studies on the determinants of central-bank independence. The second column shows the measure(s) of independence used. The third and fourth columns present the sample of countries and the estimation period, respectively. The last column contains the economic and political variables examined in the studies.

The Equilibrium Level of Unemployment

The first determinant of central-bank independence may be the average employment-motivated inflationary bias in a country. This inflationary

41

TABLE 8

EMPIRICAL STUDIES ON THE DETERMINANTS OF CENTRAL-BANK INDEPENDENCE

Study	Measure(s) Used	Countries	Estimation Period	Variables Examined
Cukierman (1992)	LVAU; LVAW	14 middle-income	1972–79; 1980–89	Political instability (party and regime)
Posen (1993a)	LVAU	17 industrial	1950–89	Financial opposition to inflation
De Haan and Siermann (1994)	TOR	43 developing	1950–89; subperiods	Political instability (party and regime)
Moser (1994)	Average of GMT and LVAW	22 industrial	1967–90	Political system index (PSI); standard deviation of output growth
Cukierman and Webb (1995)	Political vulnerability	64 industrial and developing	1950–89	Four types of political instability (high- and low-level)
De Haan and Van 't Hag (1995)	GMT; LVAU; SUMLV	19 (16) industrial 21 (18) industrial 17 industrial 16 (13) industrial	1980–88 1980–89 1950–98 1900–40	NAIRU; government debt ratio; frequency of (significant) government changes; banking supervision; universal banking; very long-term inflation
Eijffinger and Schaling (1995)	AL; ES; GMT; LVAU (latent-variables method)	19 industrial	1960–93 (for NAIRU: 1960–88)	NAIRU; relative number of years of socialist (left-wing) government; variance of output growth; compensation of employees paid by resident producers

NOTE: AL = Alesina; BP = Bade-Parkin; ES = Eijffinger-Schaling; GMT = Grilli, Masciandaro, and Tabellini; LVAU = Cukierman's unweighted legal-independence index; LVAW = Cukierman's weighted legal-independence index; QVAW = Cukierman's weighted index based on a questionnaire; SUMLV = Cukierman's sum of sixteen legal variables; TOR = the turnover rate of central-bank governors.

bias can be approximated empirically by the equilibrium or natural rate of unemployment.[31] Cukierman (1994) shows that the larger the average employment-motivated inflationary bias in a country, the higher will be the costs for the government to override the central bank and the more independent the central bank will be.[32] Because in the case of nominal-wage contracts, unexpected inflation has positive effects on the levels of both production and employment, a higher equilibrium or natural rate of unemployment implies that surprise inflation is more valuable for the government.[33]

De Haan and Van 't Hag (1995) have tested this hypothesis, using two measures of Cukierman (LVAU and SUMLV)[34] and the index of Grilli, Masciandaro, and Tabellini (GMT). Proxies for inflationary bias are the equilibrium rate of unemployment, as estimated by Layard, Nickell, and Jackman (1991) for nineteen industrial countries, and the difference between the actual and the equilibrium rate of unemployment during the 1980s. In simple cross-country regressions with each measure of central-bank independence as a dependent variable, the coefficients of both proxies prove to be insignificant. Eijffinger and Schaling (1995) employ a latent-variables method to distinguish between the actual (legal) and optimal degree of central-bank independence in these countries. As measures for actual central-bank autonomy, the indices of Alesina (AL), Grilli, Masciandaro, and Tabellini (GMT), Eijffinger and Schaling (ES), and Cukierman (LVAU) are chosen. Eijffinger and Schaling also find an insignificant coefficient for the natural rate of

[31] In this case, the natural rate of unemployment is referred to as the "nonaccelerating inflation rate of unemployment" (NAIRU). This implies that the desired unemployment rate is being held constant and, thus, that the inflationary bias is driven by the difference between the desired and natural unemployment rate.

[32] Similarly, Eijffinger and Schaling (1995) suggest that the higher the natural rate of unemployment, the higher will be the optimal degree of central-bank independence. The intuition behind this proposition is as follows. A higher natural rate of unemployment leads to a higher time-consistent rate of inflation and, consequently, to an increase in society's credibility problem. Hence, with an unaltered relative weight placed on inflation stabilization, as opposed to unemployment stabilization, the monetary authorities' commitment to fighting inflation will now be too low to be effective.

[33] Schaling (1995) gives an analysis with an endogenous NAIRU and its implications for the optimal degree of central-bank independence.

[34] The index SUMLV measures the *total* score of sixteen legal variables of Cukierman (1992) with respect to the appointment, dismissal, and term of office of the central-bank president; the solution for conflicts between the government and the central bank; the policy goals of the central bank; and the legal limitations for the government to borrow from the central bank.

unemployment. We may therefore conclude that empirical studies provide no support for any relation between the equilibrium or natural rate of unemployment and the degree of central-bank independence.

Government Debt

The stock of government debt is another potential determinant of central-bank independence. The larger the sum the government wants to borrow on the capital market, the more weight will be placed on lower inflationary expectations and, thus, on lower nominal capital-market interest rates. The benefits of a once-and-for-all reduction of the real value of government debt by unexpected inflation do not outweigh (in this case) the costs of permanently higher interest payments as a consequence of lower credibility. Cukierman (1994) argues that the larger the debt, the more likely it is that politicians will delegate authority to the central bank and the more independent the central bank will be. This hypothesis is empirically investigated by De Haan and Van 't Hag (1995) for several measures of independence (LVAU, SUMLV, and GMT) for the 1980–89 period. Using gross government debt as a percentage of GDP in their regression analysis, these authors find no significant coefficient for the debt ratio.

Political Instability

The influence of political instability on central-bank independence is, at first sight, less obvious than the impact of the other factors discussed above.[35] It can be argued that when politicians in office are faced with a greater probability that they will be removed from office, they have a stronger interest in delegating authority to the central bank (an apolitical institution) in order to restrict the range of policy actions available to the opposition should the latter come into office. This implies that greater political instability leads to a more independent central bank. Conversely, it can be argued that the incumbent politicians will fortify their hold on the central bank if there is a greater probability of government change and will eventually overrule central-bank decisionmaking. The short-term benefits of surprise inflation may thereby exceed their long-term costs. It follows that greater political instability will result in a more dependent central bank.

---

[35] For the effect of political instability on variables such as (the increase of) the stock of government debt and seigniorage, see Persson and Svensson (1989), Alesina and Tabellini (1990), Tabellini and Alesina (1990), Cukierman, Edwards, and Tabellini (1992) and De Haan and Sturm (1994b).

Cukierman (1992) argues that it is possible to combine both hypotheses into a single, internally consistent theory. In countries with a sufficiently high degree of national consensus, greater political instability may be associated with increased independence of the central bank, whereas the reverse may apply for countries with a relatively low level of national consensus. Cukierman has tested this combined hypothesis, using two indices of political instability constructed by Haggard et al. (1991) for fourteen middle-income countries during the 1970s and 1980s. The first index, *party political instability*, measures the degree of political instability under a given regime and refers to a relatively high level of national consensus. The second index, *regime political instability*, reflects the degree of political instability in the case of a relatively low level of national consensus. Regression analysis by Cukierman for legal-independence measures during the 1972–79 and 1980–89 periods shows that the indices have the expected signs. This result may be questioned, however, because legal measures of central-bank independence may not be a very good proxy for actual central-bank independence in developing countries. Two studies have recently employed nonlegal measures of central-bank independence.

Cukierman and Webb (1995) use a measure of political vulnerability, the percentage of times that political transition is followed by a change of central-bank governor, as a dependent variable, and four types of political instability as explanatory variables for a mixture of industrial and developing countries during the 1950–89 period. Only high-level political instability (a change in regime) and the dummy for developing countries prove to be significant.

De Haan and Siermann (1994) have estimated the relation between central-bank independence and political instability by using data provided by Cukierman, Webb, and Neyapti (1992) on the turnover rate of central-bank governors (TOR) for forty-three developing countries over four periods (1950–59, 1960–71, 1972–79 and 1980–89). Proxies for political stability are the number of regular and irregular government transfers (*coups d'état*). In the regressions of De Haan and Siermann, only the variable "*coups*" exerts a significantly negative effect on central-bank independence.

In a recent study, Cukierman (1994, p. 65) states that the greater the political instability, the higher will be the degree of central-bank independence, "provided political polarization is sufficiently large." The intuition behind this proposition is that the ruling party prefers a more independent central bank when the prospects for the party's reelection are slim. As the probability of reelection shrinks, the benefits of central-bank independence increase in terms of restricting public expenditure by the opposition party. Cukierman's hypothesis is investigated by De Haan and Van 't Hag (1995) for three different measures of central-bank autonomy (LVAU, SUMLV, and GMT) during the 1970s and 1980s using regression analysis based on industrial countries. De Haan and Van 't Hag use both the frequency of government changes and the frequency of significant government changes (that is, the case of another party or coalition coming to office) as indices of political instability. For the first index, all three measures of central-bank independence show a significant, negative relationship; for the second index, the results are not significant.

We may conclude from the above that the empirical results regarding political instability are mixed. The various studies are hard to compare properly, however, because they refer to different groups of countries, diverging measures of central-bank independence, and various proxies for political instability.

The Supervision of Financial Institutions

The supervision of financial institutions ("banking supervision") may also be a political-economic determinant of the degree of central-bank independence. Goodhart and Schoenmaker (1993) analyze the supervision of financial institutions in twenty-six countries. Table 9 shows that, in approximately half of these countries, the central bank is also responsible for supervising the financial institutions and, thus, that the function of supervisory agency is combined (C) with the responsibility for monetary policy. In the other half of the countries, responsibility is separated (S) between the central bank and the ministry of finance or other supervisory agencies.

It may be inferred from Table 9, in conjunction with Table 2, that the supervision of financial institutions has little impact on the independence of central banks. In fact, practical policy in these countries does not allow clear-cut conclusions regarding the relation between combined or separated responsibility for financial supervision and monetary policy, on the one hand, and central-bank independence, on the other. We shall thus discuss the main arguments for and against a separation of responsibilities, according to Goodhart and Schoenmaker (1993).

The first argument in favor of separating financial supervision and the conduct of monetary policy is the possibility of a conflict of interest in having a single institution manage both activities. A central bank that is responsible for supervision of the financial system and, thus, also for failures of financial institutions, might be tempted to avoid such failures

46

TABLE 9

CENTRAL BANKS AND THE SUPERVISION OF FINANCIAL INSTITUTIONS

Country	Supervisory Agency			Combined or Separated
	Central Bank	Finance Ministry	Other Entities	
Australia	X	—	—	C
Austria	—	X	—	S
Belgium	—	—	Banking and Finance Commission	S
Brazil	X	—	—	C
Canada	—	X	—	S
Denmark	—	—	Finance Inspectorate (Industry Ministry)	S
Finland	X	X	—	S
France	X	—	Commission Bancaire	C
Germany	—	—	Bundesaufsichtsamt für das Kreditwesen	S
Greece	X	—	—	C
Hong Kong	X	—	—	C
Ireland	X	—	—	C
Italy	X	—	—	C
Japan	X	X	—	S
Luxembourg	X	—	—	C
Netherlands	X	—	—	C
New Zealand	X	—	—	C
Norway	—	X	—	S
Philippines	X	—	—	C
Portugal	X	—	—	C
Spain	X	—	—	C
Sweden	—	—	Swedish Financial Supervisory Authority	S
Switzerland	—	—	Federal Banking Commission	S
United Kingdom	X	—	—	C
United States	X	—	Comptroller of the Currency; FDIC; state governments	S
Venezuela	—	—	Superintendency of Banks	S

SOURCE: Goodhart and Schoenmaker, "Institutional Separation" (1993).

by admitting lower (money-market) interest rates or higher money growth than would be desirable from the perspective of price stability.[36] A

---

[36] Goodhart and Schoenmaker (1993) refer to the recent savings and loan crisis in the United States and its influence on the policy of the Federal Reserve as an example. It is also stated that the Federal Reserve is smoothing interest rates to encourage financial stability (Cukierman, 1992, chap. 7).

separation of responsibilities may, therefore, increase the monetary autonomy of the central bank. A second reason to separate the authority on financial stability from that on monetary stability is the bad publicity usually associated with failures or rescue operations. Unfavorable publicity might harm the reputation of the central bank in its function as a supervisory agency. A loss of reputation might then affect the credibility of monetary policy. Separating responsibilities can, therefore, support the independence of the central bank in practice.

Several arguments may also be made against a separation of financial supervision and the conduct of monetary policy. First, the central bank plays a crucial role in the smooth operation of the payments system and its associated financial risks. To limit these risks, the central bank will (reasonably) wish to supervise and to regulate the participants of the payments system. In addition, the central bank functions as a "lender of last resort" for the financial system; in this capacity, it has the task of instantly supplying sufficient liquidity in the event of structural liquidity problems, or even in the case of rescue operations. This, then, argues for combining financial and monetary responsibility.

De Beaufort Wijnholds and Hoogduin (1994) distinguish between general, or macroeconomic, supervision, and specific, or microeconomic, supervision. These authors consider the arguments for a separation of responsibilities—the potential conflict of interest, for example—to be applicable only to microeconomic supervision, because of the close contacts of the central bank with individual banks. They conclude that it appears possible to maintain central-bank autonomy both when microeconomic (prudential) supervision and monetary policy are separated and when they are combined. The choice between separation and combination depends on the structure of the banking system and the conduct of monetary policy in the country, both of which are associated with the relative size of the economy. In smaller open industrial countries with an exchange-rate target (for example, the Netherlands), the probability of a conflict of interest between the two activities seems to be considerably lower than in the case of large industrial countries with a monetary target (such as Germany).[37]

Empirical evidence on the relation between financial supervision and central-bank independence provides no uniform conclusion. Heller (1991) compares the average rate of inflation (as a proxy of the degree

---

[37] The explanation of this could be that an exchange-rate target is more visible than a monetary target and therefore expresses a stronger commitment of the central bank (Herrendorf, 1995).

of central-bank independence) of countries with central banks that have either no responsibility, partial responsibility, or complete responsibility for financial supervision. He finds that central banks without any supervisory authority generate the lowest inflation, and that those with complete supervisory authority generate the highest inflation. Heller consequently favors a separation of responsibilities. De Haan and Van 't Hag (1995), by contrast, find no empirical relation between two of the three different measures of independence and an index (from Posen, 1993a) measuring the degree of banking supervision—an index that also includes the central-bank restrictions on lending rates and on the amount of bank credit permitted to the private sector. For only one measure of independence do these authors find a significant, negative relation with the index for the degree of banking supervision. Their result also contrasts with the view put forward by Posen, to which we now turn.

Financial Opposition to Inflation

Posen (1993a, 1993b) advocates a new view of monetary policy and central-bank independence that are, in his opinion, determined by the degree of financial opposition to inflation and by the effectiveness of the financial sector to mobilize—through the political system—its opposition to inflation. According to Posen, the causal relation between central-bank independence and low inflation is illusory, and central-bank autonomy has no noticeable effect on cross-country differences in inflation rates. Posen argues that a third factor exists that explains the negative correlation between central-bank independence and the level of inflation. This factor is the financial opposition to inflation (FOI) within a country.

Posen asserts that monetary policy is driven by a coalition of political interests in society, because central banks will be prepared to take strong anti-inflationary actions only when there is a coalition of interests politically capable of protecting their anti-inflationary policy. In industrial countries, the financial sector represents such a coalition. Posen therefore develops a measure of "effective financial opposition to inflation" to predict both the degree of central-bank independence and the rate of inflation in the various countries.[38] Posen tested four propositions regarding indicators that explain and measure financial opposition to inflation:

---

[38] As stated by Posen (1993a, p. 47), "This implies as well that *CB independence and low rates of inflation should occur together, without a causal link between them,* because they both are reflections of effective FOI."

(1) Countries with financial sectors that have universal banking are expected to have a stronger financial opposition to inflation than those without such sectors

(2) Countries with less regulatory power (supervision) of the central bank over the financial sector are expected to have more financial opposition to inflation.

(3) Countries with federal systems of government are expected to have a more effective financial opposition to inflation.

(4) Countries with less fractionalization of the political party system are expected to have a more influential financial opposition to inflation.

According to Posen (1993a), these indicators constitute the ultimate determinants of central-bank independence and the level of inflation. He claims to have found clear statistical evidence that supports a causal link between financial opposition to inflation, on the one hand, and central-bank independence (Cukierman's LVAU) and lower inflation rates, on the other, for the 1950–89 period. De Haan and Van 't Hag (1995), however, have tested Posen's proposition on universal banking by means of a dummy variable for the presence (1) or absence (0) of a universal banking system. For only one of the three independence indices did they find a significant, positive relation with the dummy for universal banking. As explained above, these authors report a similar finding with respect to the relation between prudential supervision and central-bank independence. It seems, therefore, that Posen's conclusion is sensitive to the measure of central-bank independence used.

Cukierman (1992) states that countries with broad financial markets and a substantial amount of financial intermediation are more likely to grant high levels of independence to their central banks.[39] He argues that possible disruptions as a result of less central-bank autonomy and more inflation (uncertainty) in the process of intermediation between savings and investment are proportional to the size of the financial sector in a country. As a result, countries with large financial markets are more likely to have more independent central banks than are those with narrow financial markets. This conclusion is supported, according to Cukierman, by a comparison of the size of financial markets and the ranking of central banks by overall independence—for industrial countries, LVAU, and for developing countries, LVAU and TOR, during the 1980s. Countries with well-developed financial markets (for

---

[39] The broadness of financial markets and the degree of financial intermediation are, of course, strongly associated with the depth of capital markets (Cukierman (1992).

example, France, Germany, the United Kingdom, and the United States) have relatively independent central banks, whereas those with narrow (internal) financial markets (most developing countries) have relatively dependent central banks. Nevertheless, we believe that a two-way causal relationship exists between the size of financial markets and independence—that is, that high autonomy and low inflation will also foster the development of financial markets.

Public Opposition to Inflation

Another important determinant of central-bank independence is public support for the objective of price stability or, analogous to the former determinant, public opposition to inflation.[40] It is quite obvious that this determinant should not be analyzed separately from the financial opposition to inflation as defined by Posen (1993a, 1993b), but that it has a much broader meaning. The experience of the public with extremely high inflation or even hyperinflation in the past is generally seen as the reason for vehement public opposition to inflation. This implies that a two-way causal relationship may exist between central-bank independence and the level of inflation: an independent central bank may foster low inflation in the medium and long run, but high inflation may result in the very long run in the creation of an autono-mous central bank. There seems to be a threshold value for the level of inflation above which public opposition to inflation in a country will be mobilized and taken into account by the politicians. Cukierman (1992) argues, however, that inflation, when sufficiently sustained, will erode central-bank independence. Society becomes accustomed to inflation (wages, for instance, are indexed), thereby reducing opposition to inflation and public pressure for an independent central bank.

De Haan and Van 't Hag (1995) use cross-country ordinary least-squares (OLS) regressions (with the average level of inflation between 1900 and 1940 as an explanatory variable) of three different measures of central-bank independence in industrial countries to show that a significant positive relationship exists between very long-term inflation and independence.

Referring to the medium and long term, Eijffinger and Schaling (1995), use their game-theoretical model to arrive at the proposition

---

[40] See, in this respect, Neumann (1991), Bofinger (1992), Debelle (1993), Issing (1993, 1994), Eijffinger (1994), and Fischer (1994). Issing (1993, p. 18) notes that "it is no coincidence that it is the Germans, with their experience of two hyperinflations in the 20th century, who have opted for an independent central bank which is committed to price stability."

that the stronger society's preferences are for unemployment stabilization relative to inflation stabilization, the higher will be the optimal
degree of central-bank independence. The underlying intuition of this
proposition is as follows. If society becomes more concerned with
unemployment, the time-consistent rate of inflation rises. Society's
credibility problem therefore becomes more pressing. With an unaltered
relative weight placed on inflation stabilization, the balance between
credibility and flexibility needs to be adjusted in favor of an increased
commitment of the authorities to fight inflation. Eijffinger and Schaling
test this proposition, using the number of years of socialist- (left-wing)
dominated government over the total period studied as a proxy for
society's preference for unemployment stabilization over inflation
stabilization. They find a positive, though not significant, relation
between the optimal degree of central-bank independence and society's
preferences for unemployment stabilization over inflation stabilization.

In general, the conclusion may be drawn that central-bank independence is strongly associated with society's fundamental support for the
objective of price stability. Notwithstanding the theoretical and empirical
arguments for central-bank autonomy, however, not every society and,
thus, not every government will be prepared to accept such an independent position for its central bank.

Other Determinants

Recent literature on the determinants of central-bank independence also
mentions economic and political factors that cannot be categorized under
the headings given above. We discuss these determinants briefly here.

Moser (1994) tries to identify the conditions under which transferring
monetary policy to an independent central bank is credible. His model
analyzes the interaction between a central bank and two political
decisionmaking bodies. Delegation is credible only if there are at least
two veto players in the legislative process and if they disagree to some
extent about monetary policy. Moser constructs a political-system index
that reflects differences in the ability of the political systems to make a
commitment.[41] Controlling for a potential effect of external real
shocks, he reports a significant, positive effect of his political-system
index on an average of the GMT and LVAU measures of independence

---

[41] This political-system index ranges from a value of 1 for pure unicameral legislatures
and bicameral legislatures with both chambers being equally composed, to a value of 4
for strong bicameral systems with equal power and unequal composition. The last are
characterized by a high degree of federalism.

for twenty-two industrial countries during the 1967–90 period. He finds that countries with extensive checks and balances are associated with more independent central banks.

Based on their game-theoretical model, Eijffinger and Schaling (1995) propose that the higher the variance of productivity shocks, the lower will be the optimal degree of central-bank independence. The intuition for this argument is that if the variance of productivity shocks increases, the economy will, *ceteris paribus*, become more unstable, and the need for an active stabilization policy will thus become greater. With an unaltered relative weight placed on inflation stabilization, the balance between credibility and flexibility will shift toward greater monetary accommodation by the authorities. Eijffinger and Schaling test this proposition with the variance of annual output growth to approximate the variance of productivity shocks. Distinguishing legal independence from optimal independence with a latent-variables method, they find the expected negative relation between the variance of productivity shocks and the optimal degree of central-bank independence for nineteen industrial countries for the 1960–93 period. The coefficient is, however, insignificant.

Eijffinger and Schaling (1995) state, in addition, that the steeper the slope of the Phillips curve, the higher will be the optimal degree of central-bank independence. If the slope of the Phillips curve increases, the benefits of unanticipated inflation will rise. It therefore becomes more tempting for the government to inflate the economy, and, *ceteris paribus*, society's credibility problem gains in importance. With constant relative weights on inflation stabilization, the balance between credibility and flexibility needs to shift toward greater commitment to fight inflation. This proposition is tested by Eijffinger and Schaling, using the compensation of employees paid by resident producers as a ratio of GDP as a proxy for the slope of the Phillips curve. Using the latent-variables method, a significant positive relation is found between the slope of the Phillips curve and the optimal degree of central-bank independence for nineteen industrial countries for the 1960–93 period.

6 CONCLUDING COMMENTS

This survey has discussed the theoretical and empirical literature on central-bank autonomy. Its review of the various measures of central-bank independence makes it clear that all of them have their limitations. It is also apparent that the concept of central-bank independence used in most theoretical studies diverges somewhat from the proxies of central-bank independence used in the empirical literature. Further research on the reliability of, and alternatives for, the various measures is clearly needed.

Is "the only good central bank one that can say no to the politicians"? Although an independent central bank is neither a sufficient nor necessary condition for price stability, we must agree with the theoretical literature and previous empirical studies that a country with an independent central bank will, *ceteris paribus*, have a lower rate of inflation than will a country where politicians can steer the central bank's policy. In principle, then, because attaining lower inflation rates bears no costs in terms of lower long-term economic growth, we can answer the question in the affirmative. The tendency that is currently apparent in many countries toward greater central-bank autonomy should therefore be regarded positively. Nevertheless, some important caveats are in order.

First, the absence of a significant influence of the various measures of central-bank independence on the rate of economic growth may also be interpreted in a less positive way. Stable monetary policy aimed at low inflation is usually considered to be an important condition for sustainable economic growth. Most empirical studies, however, show that central-bank autonomy does not enhance economic growth and employment. Moreover, there is no proof that countries with relatively independent central banks have lower costs of disinflation than those with more dependent central banks. Indeed, most studies suggest that central-bank independence is associated with higher disinflation costs.

Second, the tendency toward central-bank autonomy may conflict with the goal of accountability for central banks. In the short run, there seems to be a trade-off between central-bank independence and accountability. We believe, however, that such a trade-off does not exist in the long run. A central bank that continuously conducts policy that lacks broad political support will sooner or later be overridden. At the same time, our conclusion underscores the importance of broad public support for a central bank's autonomy and its anti-inflationary policy. Although the determinants of central-bank independence have only recently been investigated, current research leads us to conclude that every society gets the central bank it deserves. This conclusion implies also that simply changing central-bank law is insufficient to guarantee structurally lower levels of inflation. Only in an environment of widespread and overwhelming support for anti-inflation policy pursued by an independent central bank will inflation effectively be reduced. The policy to give the Banque de France a more independent position, for example, is backed by both the government and the opposition parties. After the failed experiment of an expansionary policy in France at the beginning of the 1980s, governments of alternating political composition have all supported a monetary policy strongly focused on Germany. In such circumstances, the development toward an independent central bank is a logical step.

It is doubtful, however, that there is enough support for a restrictive monetary policy in some of the Southern and Eastern European countries for this to occur. More autonomy for central banks in these countries will thus be insufficient to guarantee a permanently lower level of inflation.

APPENDIX A: LEGAL MEASURES OF CENTRAL-BANK INDEPENDENCE

Alesina's (1988, 1989) legal measure of central-bank independence is based primarily on an unpublished paper by Bade and Parkin (1988) that classifies central banks into four groups. Bade and Parkin give a score of 1 to the least independent banks and a score of 4 to the most independent banks. They apply the following criteria in analyzing central-bank laws:

- Is the central bank the final authority?
- Are more than half of the policy-board appointments made independently of the government?
- Is there no government official (with or without voting power) on the bank policy board?

For central banks with the highest degree of autonomy, all three questions are answered in the affirmative. Country placements, from those having the least independent central banks (1) to the most independent central banks (4), are: (1) Australia; (2) Belgium, Canada, France, Italy, the Netherlands, Sweden, and the United Kingdom; (3) Japan and the United States; and (4) Germany and Switzerland. The numerical values of the Alesina index are identical to those of the Bade-Parkin index, except for the case of Italy. The difference in evaluation for Italy is based on the "divorce" (*divorzio*) of the Italian treasury and the Banca d'Italia in 1981, after which the Banca d'Italia was no longer obliged to absorb the excess supply of short-term treasury bills. This step decreased the scope for monetary financing of government deficits and increased the independence of the Banca d'Italia. Alesina adds Denmark, New Zealand, Norway, and Spain to the classification, using information from Fair (1980) and Masciandaro and Tabellini (1988).

The index of Grilli, Masciandaro, and Tabellini (1991) consists of two parts: political independence and economic independence. The first measures the capacity to choose the final goal of monetary policy; the second indicates the capacity of the central bank to choose independently its instruments of monetary policy. The degree of political independence is determined using eight criteria:

(1) Is the governor not appointed by the government?
(2) Is the governor appointed for more than five years?
(3) Are all policy-board members not appointed by the government?
(4) Is the policy board appointed for more than five years?
(5) Is there no mandatory participation of a government representative on the policy board?
(6) Is government approval of monetary policy required?
(7) Are there statutory requirements that the bank must pursue monetary stability among its goals?
(8) Are there legal provisions that strengthen the bank's position in case of conflict with the government?

Germany and the Netherlands score highest on this political-independence index. The numerical coding for economic independence is determined on the basis of the following eight items:

(1) Is the direct-credit facility not automatic?
(2) Is the direct-credit facility based on the market interest rate?
(3) Is the direct-credit facility temporary?
(4) Is the direct-credit facility of a limited amount?
(5) Does the central bank not participate in the primary market for public debt?
(6) Is the discount rate determined by the central bank?
(7) Is banking supervision not entrusted to the central bank?
(8) Is banking supervision not entrusted to the central bank alone?

Again, Germany appears to have the most independent central bank.[42]

With respect to the last two criteria of the economic-independence measure, some additional comments are in order. In the debate about whether central banks should or should not be entrusted with prudential supervising powers, various arguments have been advanced to support both views (Roll et al., 1993; De Beaufort Wijnholds and Hoogduin, 1994). The most important argument in favor of separating the functions of monetary policymaking and prudential supervision is based on the fear that the central bank's anti-inflationary stance will be undermined by a large injection of liquidity aimed at keeping one or more important financial institutions afloat. Even if banking supervision is performed by another agency, however, the central bank will have to

---

[42] According to Alesina and Grilli (1992), the ECB receives exactly the same scores as the Bundesbank, applying both the political- and economic-independence measures.

intervene if one of the larger banks goes bankrupt. De Haan and Sturm (1994a) therefore conclude that either entrusting or not entrusting a central bank with banking supervision has little impact on its independence.

Eijffinger and Schaling (1992, 1993a) develop an alternative measure for central-bank autonomy on the basis of the following three features:[43]

(1) Is the bank the sole final policy authority; that is, is this authority shared, or is the authority entrusted completely to the government?
(2) Is there no government official (with or without voting power) on the bank policy board?
(3) Are more than half of the policy-board appointments made independently of the government?

If the central bank has sole responsibility for monetary policy, a country gets a double score. If it has joint responsibility, the country gets a normal score. If only the government has responsibility, it gets no score. In case of an affirmative answer to questions 2 and 3, a country receives a normal score. Eijffinger and Schaling add one to the total score so that the least independent central bank receives a score of 1, and the most independent bank receives a score of 5.

Cukierman's (LVAU) measure is also based on the interpretation of various elements of central-bank laws. These legal characteristics are grouped into four clusters, relating to:

(1) The appointment, dismissal, and term of office of the chief executive officer (CEO) of the bank, usually the governor
   (a) What is the term of office (TOO)?
   (b) Who appoints the CEO (APP)?
   (c) Who dismisses the CEO (DISS)?
   (d) May the CEO hold other offices in government (OFF)?
(2) Policy formulation
   (a) Who formulates monetary policy (MONPOL)?
   (b) Who has the final word in the resolution of conflict (CONF)?
   (c) What is the bank's role in the government's budgetary process (ADV)?
(3) The objectives of the central bank (OBJ)

[43] Recently, Eijffinger and Van Keulen (1995) extended their sample of twelve countries by another eleven countries. Except for Denmark, these eleven have adjusted their central-bank laws, mostly during the last ten years.

(4) Limitations on the ability of the central bank to lend to the public sector, specifically with regard to:
(a) advances (LLA)
(b) securitized lending (LLS)
(c) terms of lending (LDEC)
(d) potential borrowers from the bank (LWIDTH)
(e) the definition of limits (LTYPE)
(f) maturity of loans (LMAT)
(g) the interest rate that is being applied (LINT)
(h) whether or not the central bank is prohibited from buying or selling government securities in the primary market (LPRIM)

For each of these variables, Cukierman discerns various possibilities, which receive a numerical coding from 0 to 1. The following possibilities exist for the third cluster: price stability is the primary or only objective, and in case of conflict, the central bank has the final word (1); price stability is the only objective (0.8); price stability is one goal, with other compatible objectives (0.6); price stability is one goal, together with other, potentially conflicting objectives (0.4); the charter does not state any objective (0.2); and, finally: stated objectives do not include price stability (0).

To assess the overall independence of a central bank, Cukierman computes two alternative indices: an unweighted index (LVAU), calculated as a simple average of the codings of the variables obtained in a first round of aggregation, and a weighted index. The first round of aggregation includes the following procedure. The variables in the first cluster are aggregated into a single variable, using the unweighted mean of the various criteria. The three criteria in the second cluster are combined into a new variable by computing a weighted mean (the weights are 0.25, 0.5, and 0.25, respectively). The last four variables in the fourth cluster are aggregated into a single variable, using the unweighted mean. This gives a total of eight variables (the three new ones and the five remaining variables). Cukierman's index, LVAU, is the unweighted average of these variables. Cukierman, Webb, and Neyapti (1992) present a weighted average of these variables (LVAW).

As explained in Chapter 3, a crucial element in determining legal independence is the interpretation of central-bank laws. For illustrative purposes, Table A1 shows Cukierman's various codings, our numerical codings (in parentheses), and our interpretation of the Dutch Bank Law. This table shows, that in our view, the Dutch central bank is much more independent than Cukierman's coding suggests.

TABLE A1

CUKIERMAN'S LEGAL VARIABLES: THE DUTCH CASE

Variable	Cukierman's Coding	Interpretation	Comments	Authors' Coding
TOO	0.75	$8 > \text{TOO} > 6$	Board members appointed for seven years; appointment is renewable	—
APP	0.00	CEO appointed by minister of finance	Correct; but on the basis of a list drafted by the governing and supervisory boards of the bank and containing only two names	0.75
DISS	0.17	Dismissal for policy reasons at discretion of executive branch	Only if the minister gives a "directive" that is rejected by the governing board; such a directive has never been given	0.83
OFF	1.00	CEO prohibited from holding other office	Correct	—
MONPOL	0.33	Central bank has only advisory capacity	Incorrect; central bank has full freedom in formulating and implementing monetary policy, except for the (theoretical) possibility pointed out above	1.00
CONF	0.20	Government has final authority in case of conflict but is subject to process and protest by central bank	Correct; but this process has never occurred, because it is linked to the "directive" procedure	—
ADV	0.00	Central bank has no active role in the formulation of government's budget	Correct; but may have nothing to do with central-bank autonomy; it can be argued that involvement by the central bank might threaten its independence	—

OBJ	0.80	Price stability mentioned as only goal	Not entirely correct; the wording of the law also implies external stability	—
LLA	0.67	Relatively strict limits (cash amount)	Correct; collateral is necessary	—
LLS	0.00	No limits	Correct; but this type of credit is not provided	—
LDEC	0.00	Executive branch decides the terms	Incorrect; the law specifies the terms	—
LWIDTH	1.00	Only central government can borrow	Not entirely correct; Amsterdam and Social Insurance Bank may also borrow	—
LTYPE	1.00	Limits specified as cash amount	Correct with respect to article 20 of the Bank Law; additional liquidity may be provided, but is limited to a percentage of total government revenues	—
LMAT	0.00	No upper bound	Incorrect; maturity is limited to one year	0.66
LINT	0.00	No interest-rate charge	Correct	—
LPRIM	0.00	Not prohibited from buying government securities in primary market	Correct	—

NOTE: TOO = term of office; APP = who appoints the CEO?; DISS = who dismisses the CEO?; OFF = may the CEO hold other offices in government?; MONPOL = who formulates monetary policy; CONF = who has the final word in the resolution of conflict; ADV = what is the bank's role in the government's budgetary process; OBJ = objectives of the central bank; LLA = limitations on advances to public sector by central bank; LLS = limitations on securitized lending to public sector by central bank; LDEC = limitations on terms of lending to public sector by central bank; LWIDTH = limitations on potential borrowers from the central bank; LTYPE = how limits are defined; LMAT = maturity of loans; LINT = which interest rate is being applied; LPRIM = is the central bank prohibited from buying or selling government securities in the primary market.

APPENDIX B: EMPIRICAL RESEARCH ON THE CONSEQUENCES OF CENTRAL-BANK INDEPENDENCE

This appendix summarizes in tabular form empirical research on the relation between central-bank independence and various economic variables. Table B1 presents all the studies of which we are aware. Table B2 summarizes the conclusions of studies dealing with the relation between central-bank independence and inflation. Table B3 reviews evidence on the relation between central-bank independence and economic growth. And Table B4 presents studies on the relation between central-bank independence and other economic variables.

TABLE B1

EMPIRICAL STUDIES ON THE CONSEQUENCES OF CENTRAL-BANK INDEPENDENCE

Study	Measure(s) Used	Countries	Period	Variables Examined
Bade and Parkin (1988)	BP	12 industrial	1972–86	Inflation, inflation variability
Alesina (1988, 1989)	AL	16 industrial	1973–85	Inflation, inflation variability
Grilli, Masciandaro, and Tabellini (1991)	GMT	18 industrial	1950–89 and subperiods	Inflation, budget deficit, output growth, and variability of growth
Cukierman (1992)	LVAW, QVAW, TOR	70 industrial and developing	1950–89 and subperiods	Inflation, central-bank credit to public sector
Cukierman, Webb, and Neyapti (1992)	LVAW, QVAW, TOR	72 industrial and developing	1950–89 and subperiods	Inflation, inflation variability, central-bank credit to public sector
De Haan and Sturm (1992)	AL, ES, GMT	14, 18, and 11 industrial	1961–87 and subperiods	Inflation, inflation variability, output growth, growth variability, budget deficit, central-bank credit to government
De Long and Summers (1992)	Average of AL and GMT	16 industrial	1955–90	Growth of output per worker
Alesina and Summers (1993)	Average of AL and GMT	16 industrial	1955–88 and 1973–88	Inflation, inflation variability, GNP growth, variability of growth, level and variance of unemployment, level and variance of interest rate
Cukierman et al. (1993)	LVAW, TOR	about 50 industrial and developing	1960–89	Per capita growth rate, private investment, productivity growth, interest rates
De Haan, Knot, and Sturm (1993)	GMT	18 industrial	1979–89	Disinflation costs
Eijffinger and Schaling (1993b)	AL, BP, ES, GMT	12 industrial	1972–91 and subsamples	Inflation, inflation variability, output growth, variability of growth
Havrilesky and Granato (1993)	AL	18 industrial	1955–87	Inflation
Pollard (1993)	Average of AL and GMT	16 industrial	1973–89	Budget deficit and variance of deficits

Study	Index/measure	Sample	Period	Variables
De Haan and Eijffinger (1994)	AL, ES, GMT, LVAU	12, 18, and 21 industrial	1972–91, 1977–81, 1982–91	Inflation, inflation variability, output growth, variability of growth
De Haan and Siermann (1994)	TOR	43 developing	1950–89	Inflation
Eijffinger, Van Rooij, and Schaling (1994)	AL, BP, EMP, ES, GMT	10 industrial	1977–90	Inflation, inflation variability, output growth, variability of growth, level and variance of interest rate
Fratianni and Huang (1994)	Average of 9 indicators	15 industrial	1960–90	Inflation, inflation variability, output growth, variability of growth
Al-Marhubi and Willett (1995)	AL, GMT, LVAW	21 industrial	1973–89	Inflation
Cargill (1995)	LVAW	20 industrial	Subperiods of 1962–91	Inflation
Cukierman and Webb (1995)	Political vulnerability	64 industrial and developing	1950–89	Inflation, inflation variability, output growth, level and variance of interest rate
Debelle and Fischer (1995)	GMT and components thereof	18 industrial	1960–92	Inflation, disinflation costs
De Haan (1995b)	Components of LVAW	21 industrial	1973–89	Inflation, inflation variability
Eijffinger and Van Keulen (1995)	AL, BP, ES, GMT	11 (3 Eastern European)	1982–93	Inflation, inflation variability
Gärtner (1995)	GMT, LVAW, average of AL and GMT	9 (16) industrial	1960–88	Disinflation costs
Walsh (1995a)	GMT, LVAW	11 EC	1973–91/92	Disinflation costs
Bleaney (1996)	LVAW	17 industrial	1973–89	Inflation, unemployment

NOTE: AL = Alesina; BP = Bade-Parkin; EMP = empirical index of central-bank independence; ES = Eijffinger-Schaling; GMT = Grilli, Masciandaro, and Tabellini; LVAU = is Cukierman's unweighted legal-independence index; LVAW = Cukierman's weighted legal-independence index; QVAW = Cukierman's weighted index based on a questionnaire; TOR = the turnover rate of central-bank governors.

TABLE B2

EMPIRICAL STUDIES ON THE RELATION BETWEEN CENTRAL-BANK INDEPENDENCE AND INFLATION

Study	Inflation	Inflation variability	Comments
Bade and Parkin (1988)	Inverse relation	No relation	—
Alesina (1988, 1989)	Inverse relation	Less partisan volatility in countries with independent central bank	Not robust (see text)
Grilli, Masciandaro, and Tabellini (1991)	Significant negative relation, except for 1950s and 1960s	—	Other variables included
Cukierman (1992)	LVAW significant for industrial countries but not for developing countries; TOR significant for developing countries	—	—
Cukierman, Webb, and Neyapti (1992)	LVAW significant for industrial countries but not for developing countries; TOR significant for developing countries	Same result as for inflation	—
De Haan and Sturm (1992)	Significant negative relation, except for 1960s	Significant negative, except for 1960s	Other variables included
Alesina and Summers (1993)	Significant negative relation	Significant negative relation	—
Eijffinger and Schaling (1993b)	Significant negative relation, except for GMT (political)	No relation, except for GMT (political)	Variance measured on monthly basis
Havrilesky and Granato (1993)	Significant negative relation	—	Measures for corporatist structure also taken into account
De Haan and Eijffinger (1994)	Significant negative relation	Mixed results	Results depending on the number of countries
De Haan and Siermann (1994)	TOR has significant positive impact on inflation	—	Political instability also taken into account

Study			
Eijffinger, Van Rooij, and Schaling (1994)	Significant negative relation, except for GMT	No relation, except for GMT	—
Fratianni and Huang (1994)	Significant negative relation	Same result as for inflation	—
Al-Marhubi and Willett (1995)	Significant negative relation	—	Measures for corporatist structure and other factors that may influence inflation also taken into account
Cargill (1995)	No robust relation	—	Statistical association is not robust and depends on countries included and regression specification
Cukierman and Webb (1995)	Political vulnerability of central bank has significant positive impact on inflation	Same result as for inflation	Political instability also included in regressions
Debelle and Fischer (1995)	Instrument independence and statutory requirement for price stability are significant, but variables relating to appointment procedures are not	—	—
De Haan (1995b)	Significant negative relation with proxy for instrument independence	Same result as for inflation	—
Eijffinger and Van Keulen (1995)	No significant relation for total sample of countries	No relation	For countries where central-bank law has been in force for more than five years, a negative association exists between independence and inflation (for GMT and ES)
Bleaney (1996)	Significant negative reaction	—	Measures for corporatist structure also taken into account

NOTE: GMT = Grilli, Masciandaro, and Tabellini; ES = Eijffinger-Schaling; LVAW = Cukierman's weighted legal-independence index; TOR = the turnover rate of central-bank governors.

TABLE B3

EMPIRICAL STUDIES ON THE RELATION BETWEEN CENTRAL-BANK INDEPENDENCE AND ECONOMIC GROWTH

Study	Economic Growth	Variability of Growth	Disinflation Costs
Grilli, Masciandaro, and Tabellini (1991)	No relation	No relation	—
De Haan and Sturm (1992)	No relation	No relation	—
De Long and Summers (1992)	Positive relation, while controlling for other factors	—	—
Alesina and Summers (1993)	No relation	No relation	—
Cukierman et al. (1993)	No relation using legal index, but significant relation using TOR	Negative relation between variability and independence proxied by TOR	—
De Haan, Knot, and Sturm (1993)	—	—	No relation
Eijffinger and Schaling (1993b)	No relation	No relation	—
De Haan and Eijffinger (1994)	No relation	No relation	—
Eijffinger, Van Rooij, and Schaling (1994)	No relation	No relation	—
Fratianni and Huang (1994)	No relation	No relation	—
Posen (1994)	—	—	Significant positive relation
Cukierman and Webb (1995)	Political vulnerability of central bank significantly inhibits growth	—	—
Debelle and Fischer (1995)	—	—	Significant positive relation
Gärtner (1995)	—	—	Significant positive relation
Walsh (1995a)	—	—	Significant positive relation

NOTE: TOR = the turnover rate of central-bank governors.

TABLE B4

EMPIRICAL STUDIES ON THE RELATION BETWEEN CENTRAL-BANK INDEPENDENCE AND OTHER ECONOMIC VARIABLES

Study	Interest Rate	Budget Deficit	Central-Bank Credit
Grilli, Masciandaro, and Tabellini (1991)	—	Negative, but insignificant, effect	—
Cukierman (1992)	—	—	TOR significant in sample including all countries
Cukierman, Webb, and Neyapti (1992)	—	—	TOR significant in sample including all countries
De Haan and Sturm (1992)	—	Mixed results (AL and GMT sometimes significant; ES not)	Only significant for GMT
Alesina and Summers (1993)	No relation, but lower variance of interest rates	—	—
Pollard (1993)	—	No significant relation with level, but significant lower variance of deficits	—
Eijffinger, Van Rooij and Schaling (1994)	Significant negative relation for AL, BP, EMP, and ES; no relation with variance (except for EMP)	—	—
Cukierman and Webb (1995)	Significant negative relation with political vulnerability of central bank	—	—

NOTE: AL = Alesina; BP = Bade-Parkin; EMP = empirical index of central-bank independence; ES = Eijffinger-Schaling; GMT = Grilli, Masciandaro, and Tabellini; TOR = the turnover rate of central-bank governors.

REFERENCES

Akhtar, M.A., and Howard Howe, "The Political and Institutional Independence of US Monetary Policy," *Banca Nazionale del Lavoro Quarterly Review*, 178 (1991), pp. 343–389.

Alesina, Alberto, "Macroeconomics and Politics," *NBER Macroeconomics Annual*, Cambridge, Mass., Cambridge University Press, 1988.

———, "Politics and Business Cycles in Industrial Democracies," *Economic Policy*, 8 (1989), pp. 55–98.

Alesina, Alberto, and Roberta Gatti, "Independent Central Banks: Low Inflation at No Cost?" *American Economic Review*, Papers and Proceedings, 85 (1995), pp. 196–200.

Alesina, Alberto, and Vittorio Grilli, "The European Central Bank: Reshaping Monetary Politics in Europe," in Matthew B. Canzoneri, Vittorio Grilli, and Paul R. Masson, eds., *Establishing a Central Bank: Issues in Europe and Lessons from the US*, Cambridge and New York, Cambridge University Press, 1992, pp. 49–77.

Alesina, Alberto, and Lawrence H. Summers, "Central Bank Independence and Macroeconomic Performance: Some Comparative Evidence," *Journal of Money, Credit, and Banking*, 25 (1993), pp. 151–162.

Alesina, Alberto, and Guido Tabellini, "Rules and Discretion with Non-Coordinated Monetary and Fiscal Policies," *Economic Inquiry*, 25 (1987), pp. 619–630.

———, "A Political Theory of Fiscal Deficits and Government Debt in a Democracy," *Review of Economic Studies*, 57 (1990), pp. 403–414.

Allen, Stuard D., "The Federal Reserve and the Electoral Cycle," *Journal of Money, Credit, and Banking*, 18 (1986), pp. 57–98.

Al-Marhubi, Fahim, and Thomas D. Willett (1995), "The Anti-Inflationary Influence of Corporatist Structures and Central Bank Independence: The Importance of the Hump Shaped Hypothesis," *Public Choice*, 84 (1996), pp. 158–162.

Andersen, Torben M., and Friedrich Schneider, "Coordination of Fiscal and Monetary Policy under Different Institutional Arrangements," *European Journal of Political Economy*, 2 (1986), pp. 169–191.

Bade, Robin, and Michael Parkin, "Central Bank Laws and Monetary Policy," University of Western Ontario, October 1988, processed.

Barro, Robert J., "Inflationary Finance under Discretion and Rules," *Canadian Journal of Economics*, 16 (1983), pp. 1–16.

———, "Inflation and Economic Growth," *Bank of England Quarterly Bulletin*, 35 (May 1995), pp. 166–176.

Barro, Robert J., and David Gordon, "Rules, Discretion and Reputation in a

Model of Monetary Policy," *Journal of Monetary Economics*, 12 (1983), pp. 101–121.

Berger, Helge, "Konjunkturpolitik im Wirtschaftwunder. Handlungsspielraume und Verhaltensmuster von Zentralbank und Regierung in den 1950er Jahren," Ph.D. diss., University of Munich, 1995.

Blake, Andrew P., and Peter F. Westaway, "Should the Bank of England be Independent?" *National Institute Economic Review*, 143 (1993), pp. 72–80.

Bleaney, Michael, "Central Bank Independence, Wage Bargaining Structure, and Macroeconomic Performance in OECD Countries," *Oxford Economic Papers*, 48 (1996), pp. 20–28.

Bofinger, Peter, "Discussion," in Matthew B. Canzoneri, Vittorio Grilli, and Paul R. Masson, eds., *Establishing a Central Bank: Issues in Europe and Lessons from the US*, Cambridge and New York, Cambridge University Press, 1992, pp. 77–80.

Bomhoff, Eduard J., *Monetary Uncertainty*, Amsterdam, New York, and Oxford, North-Holland, 1983.

Bresciani-Turroni, Constantino, *The Economics of Hyperinflation*, London, Allen and Unwin, 1953.

Buchanan, James M., and Richard M. Wagner, *Democracy in Deficit*, New York, Academic Press, 1977.

Calvo, Guillermo A., "On the Time Inconsistency of Optimal Policy in a Monetary Economy," *Econometrica*, 46 (1978), pp. 1411–1428.

Canzoneri, Matthew B., "Monetary Policy Game and the Role of Private Information," *American Economic Review*, 75 (1985), pp. 1056–1070.

Capie, Forrest H., Terence C. Mills, and Geoffrey E. Wood, "Central Bank Independence and Inflation Performance: An Exploratory Data Analysis," in Pierre L. Siklos, ed., *Varieties of Monetary Reforms: Lessons and Experiences on the Road to Monetary Union*, Dordrecht, Boston, and London, Kluwer, 1994, pp. 95–131.

Casear, Rolf, *Die Handlungsspielraum von Notenbanken*, Baden-Baden, 1981.

Chowdhury, Abdur R., "The Relationship between the Inflation Rate and its Variability: The Issues Reconsidered," *Applied Economics*, 23 (1991), pp. 993–1003.

Cukierman, Alex, *Central Bank Strategy, Credibility, and Independence*, Cambridge, Mass., MIT Press, 1992.

————, "Central Bank Independence, Political Influence and Macroeconomic Performance: A Survey of Recent Developments," *Cuadernos de Economía*, 30 (1993), pp. 271–291.

————, "Commitment through Delegation, Political Influence and Central Bank Independence," in J. Onno De Beaufort Wijnholds, Sylvester C.W. Eijffinger, and Lex H. Hoogduin, eds., *A Framework for Monetary Stability*, Dordrecht, Boston, and London, Kluwer, 1994, pp. 55–74.

————, "The Economics of Central Banking," paper presented at the Eleventh World Congress of the International Economic Association, Tunis, December 1995.

71

Cukierman, Alex, Sebastian Edwards, and Guido Tabellini, "Seignorage and Political Instability," *American Economic Review*, 82 (1992), pp. 537–555.

Cukierman, Alex, Pantelis Kalaitzidakis, Lawrence H. Summers, and Steven B. Webb, "Central Bank Independence, Growth, Investment, and Real Rates," *Carnegie-Rochester Conference Series on Public Policy*, 39 (1993), pp. 95–140.

Cukierman, Alex, Pedro Rodriguez, and Steven B. Webb, "Central Bank Autonomy and Exchange Rate Regimes: Their Effects on Monetary Accommodation and Activism," paper prepared for the Center Conference on Positive Political Economy: Theory and Evidence, Tilburg, January 23–24, 1995; forthcoming in Sylvester C.W. Eijffinger and Harry P. Huizinga, eds., *Positive Political Economy: Theory and Evidence*, Cambridge, Cambridge University Press.

Cukierman, Alex, and Paul Wachtel, "Differential Inflation Expectations and Further Thoughts on Inflation Uncertainty," *American Economic Review*, 72 (1979), pp. 508–512.

Cukierman, Alex, and Steven B. Webb, "Political Influence on the Central Bank: International Evidence," *The World Bank Economic Review*, 9 (1995), pp. 397–423.

Cukierman, Alex, Steven B. Webb, and Bilin Neyapti, "Measuring the Independence of Central Banks and Its Effects on Policy Outcomes," *The World Bank Economic Review*, 6 (1992), pp. 353–398.

De Beaufort Wijnholds, J. Onno, and Lex H. Hoogduin, "Central Bank Autonomy: Policy Issues," in J. Onno De Beaufort Wijnholds, Sylvester C.W. Eijffinger, and Lex H. Hoogduin, eds., *A Framework for Monetary Stability*, Dordrecht, Boston, and London, Kluwer, 1994, pp. 75–95.

Debelle, Guy, *Central Bank Independence: A Free Lunch?* Massachusetts Institute of Technology, Department of Economics, October 1993.

Debelle, Guy, and Stanley Fischer, "How Independent Should a Central Bank Be?" in Jeffrey C. Fuhrer, ed., *Goals, Guidelines and Constraints Facing Monetary Policymakers*, Boston, Federal Reserve Bank of Boston, Conference Series No. 38 (1995), pp. 195–221.

De Haan, Jakob, "Comment" on Alex Cukierman, Pedro Rodriguez, and Steven B. Webb, "Central Bank Autonomy and Exchange Rate Regimes: Their Effects on Monetary Accommodation and Activism," comment prepared for the Center Conference on Positive Political Economy: Theory and Evidence, Tilburg, January 23–24, 1995; forthcoming in Sylvester C.W. Eijffinger and Harry P. Huizinga, eds., *Positive Political Economy: Theory and Evidence*, Cambridge, Cambridge University Press.

——, "Why Does Central Bank Independence Yield Lower Inflation?: A Taxonomy of Arguments and Empirical Evidence," Department of Economics, University of Groningen, 1995b, processed.

De Haan, Jakob, and Sylvester C.W. Eijffinger, "De Politieke Economie van Central Bank Onafhankelijkheid: Theorie en Praktijk van Centrale Bank Autonomie," *Rotterdamse Monetaire Studies*, 13 (No. 2, 1994), pp. 1–72.

De Haan, Jakob, Klaas Knot, and Jan-Egbert Sturm, "On the Reduction of Disinflation Costs: Fixed Exchange Rates or Central Bank Independence," *Banca Nazionale del Lavoro Quarterly Review*, 187 (1993), pp. 429–443.

De Haan, Jakob, and Clemens L.J. Siermann, "Central Bank Independence, Inflation and Political Instability," Department of Economics, University of Groningen, 1994; forthcoming in *Journal of Policy Reform*.

De Haan, Jakob, and Jan-Egbert E. Sturm, "The Case for Central Bank Independence," *Banca Nazionale del Lavoro Quarterly Review*, 182 (1992), pp. 305–327; reprinted in Michael Parkin, ed., *The Theory of Inflation*, Aldershot, Edward Elgar, 1994a, pp. 627–649.

———, "Political and Institutional Determinants of Fiscal Policy in the European Community," *Public Choice*, 80 (1994b), pp. 157–172.

De Haan, Jakob, and Gert-Jan Van 't Hag, "Variation in Central Bank Independence across Countries: Some Provisional Empirical Evidence," *Public Choice*, 85 (1995), pp. 335–351.

De Long, J. Bradford, and Lawrence H. Summers, "Macroeconomic Policy and Long-Run Growth," *Federal Reserve Bank of Kansas City Economic Review*, Fourth Quarter (1992), pp. 5–29.

Eijffinger, Sylvester C.W., "A Framework for Monetary Stability—General Report," in J. Onno De Beaufort Wijnholds, Sylvester C.W. Eijffinger, and Lex H. Hoogduin, eds., *A Framework for Monetary Stability*, Dordrecht, Boston, and London, Kluwer, 1994, pp. 309–330.

———, ed., *Independent Central Banks and Economic Performance*, Cheltenham, Edward Elgar, 1996.

Eijffinger, Sylvester C.W., and Eric Schaling, "Central Bank Independence: Criteria and Indices," Research Memorandum No. 548, Department of Economics, Tilburg University, 1992, processed (a shorter version appears in *Kredit und Kapital*, Special Issue No. 13 [1995], pp. 185–216).

———, "Central Bank Independence in Twelve Industrial Countries," *Banca Nazionale del Lavoro Quarterly Review*, 184 (1993a), pp. 1–41.

———, "Central Bank Independence: Theory and Evidence," Center Discussion Paper Series No. 9325, Tilburg University, 1993b; forthcoming in *European Journal of Political Economy*.

———, "The Ultimate Determinants of Central Bank Independence," paper prepared for the Center Conference on Positive Political Economy: Theory and Evidence, Tilburg, January 23–24, 1995.

Eijffinger, Sylvester C.W., and Martÿn Van Keulen, "Central Bank Independence in Another Eleven Countries," *Banca Nazionale del Lavaro Quarterly Review*, 192 (1995), pp. 39–83.

Eijffinger, Sylvester C.W., Maarten Van Rooij, and Eric Schaling, "Central Bank Independence: A Paneldata Approach," Center Discussion Paper Series No. 9493, Tilburg University, 1994; forthcoming in *Public Choice*.

Engle, Robert F., "Estimates of the Variance of U.S. Inflation Based upon the ARCH Model," *Journal of Money, Credit, and Banking*, 15 (1983), pp. 286–301.

Evans, Martin, "Discovering the Link between Inflation Rates and Inflation Uncertainty," *Journal of Money, Credit, and Banking*, 23 (1991), pp. 169–184.

Fair, Donald E., "Relationships between Central Banks and Governments in the Determination of Monetary Policy," Société Universitaire Européenne de Recherches Financières (SUERF) Working Paper, 1980.

Fischer, Andreas M., "Central Bank Independence and Sacrifice Ratios," *Open Economies Review*, 7 (1996), pp. 5–18.

Fischer, Stanley, "The Role of Macroeconomic Factors in Economic Growth," *Journal of Monetary Economics*, 32 (1993), pp. 485–512.

———, "The Costs and Benefits of Disinflation," in J. Onno De Beaufort Wijnholds, Sylvester C.W. Eijffinger, and Lex H. Hoogduin, eds., *A Framework for Monetary Stability*, Dordrecht, Boston, and London, Kluwer, 1994, pp. 31–42.

———, "Central Bank Independence Revisited," *American Economic Review*, Papers and Proceedings, 85 (1995), pp. 201–206.

Frankel, Jeffrey A., and Katharine E. Rockett, "International Macroeconomic Policy Coordination When Policymakers Do Not Agree on the True Model," *American Economic Review*, 78 (1988), pp. 318–340.

Fratianni, Michele, and Haizhou Huang, "Reputation, Central Bank Independence and the ECB," in Pierre L. Siklos, ed., *Varieties of Monetary Reforms: Lessons and Experiences on the Road to Monetary Union*, Dordrecht, Boston, and London, Kluwer, 1994.

Friedman, Milton, "Should There Be an Independent Monetary Authority," in Leland B. Yeager, ed., *In Search of a Monetary Constitution*, Cambridge, Mass., Harvard University Press, 1962.

———, "Nobel Lecture: Inflation and Unemployment," *Journal of Political Economy*, 85 (1977), pp. 451–472.

Gärtner, Manfred, "Time-Consistent Monetary Policy under Output Persistence," Discussion Paper, University of St. Gallen, 1995.

Goodhart, Charles A.E., "Game Theory for Central Bankers: A Report to the Governor of the Bank of England," *Journal of Economic Literature*, 32 (1994), pp. 101–114.

Goodhart, Charles A.E., and Dirk Schoenmaker, "Institutional Separation between Supervisory and Monetary Authorities," paper presented at the Conference on Prudential Regulation, Supervision, and Monetary Policy, Bocconi University, Milan, 1993.

Gormley, Laurence W., and Jakob De Haan, "The Democratic Deficit of the European Central Bank," *The European Law Review*, 21 (1996), pp. 95–112.

Grilli, Vittorio, Donato Masciandaro, and Guido Tabellini, "Political and Monetary Institutions and Public Financial Policies in the Industrial Countries," *Economic Policy*, 13 (1991), pp. 341–392.

Grimes, Arthur, "The Effects of Inflation Growth: Some International Evidence," *Weltwirtschaftliches Archiv*, 127 (1991), pp. 631–644.

Haggard, Stephan, Robert Kaufman, Karim Shariff, and Steven B. Webb,

"Politics, Inflation and Government Deficits in Middle-Income Countries," Washington, D.C., World Bank, 1991, processed.

Hasse, Rolf H., *The European Central Bank: Perspectives for the Further Development of the European Monetary System*, Gütersloh, Bertelsmann Foundation, 1990.

Havrilesky, Thomas, "A Partisan Theory of Fiscal and Monetary Regimes," *Journal of Money, Credit, and Banking*, 19 (1987), pp. 308–325.

———, *The Pressures on American Monetary Policy*, Dordrecht, Boston, and London, Kluwer, 1993.

Havrilesky, Thomas, and James Granato, "Determinants of Inflationary Performance: Corporatist Structures vs Central Bank Autonomy," *Public Choice*, 76 (1993), pp. 249–261.

Heller, H. Robert, "Prudential Supervision and Monetary Policy," in Jacob A. Frenkel and Morris Goldstein, eds., *International Financial Policy: Essays in Honor of Jacques J. Polak*, Washington, D.C., International Monetary Fund, 1991.

Herrendorf, Berthold, "Exchange Rate Pegging, Transparency and Imports of Credibility," EUI Working Papers in Economics No. 95/15, European University Institute, Florence, 1995.

Hibbs, Douglas A., "Political Parties and Macroeconomic Policy," *American Political Science Review*, 23 (1977), pp. 1467–1488.

Hughes Hallett, Andrew, and Maria Luisa Petit, "Cohabitation or Forced Marriage? A Study of the Costs of Failing to Coordinate Fiscal and Monetary Policies," *Weltwirtschaftliches Archiv*, 126 (1990), pp. 662–690.

Issing, Otmar, *Central Bank Independence and Monetary Stability*, Occasional Paper No. 89, London, Institute of Economic Affairs, 1993.

———, "Monetary Policy Strategy in the EMU," in J. Onno De Beaufort Wijnholds, Sylvester C.W. Eijffinger, and Lex H. Hoogduin, eds., *A Framework for Monetary Stability*, Dordrecht, Boston, and London, Kluwer, 1994, pp. 135–148.

Jansen, Dennis W., "Does Inflation Uncertainty Affect Output Growth?— Further Evidence," *Federal Reserve Bank of St. Louis Review*, 71 (July/August 1989), pp. 43–54.

Johnson, David R., and Pierre L. Siklos, "Political Effects on Central Bank Behaviour: Some International Evidence," in Pierre Siklos, ed., *Varieties of Monetary Reforms: Lessons and Experiences on the Road to Monetary Union*, Dordrecht, Boston, and London, Kluwer, 1994, pp. 133–163.

Karras, Georgios, "Money, Inflation, and Output Growth: Does the Aggregate Demand-Aggregate Supply Model Explain the International Evidence?" *Weltwirtschaftliches Archiv*, 129 (1993), pp. 662–674.

Kennedy, Ellen, *The Bundesbank*, London, Pinter, 1991.

Kydland, Finn E., and Edward C. Prescott, "Rules Rather than Discretion: The Inconsistency of Optimal Plans," *Journal of Political Economy*, 85 (1977), pp. 473–491.

Layard, Richard, Stephen Nickell, and Richard Jackman, *Unemployment: 242 Macroeconomic Performance and the Labour Market*, Oxford and New York, Oxford University Press, 1991.

Logue, Dennis E., and Richard J. Sweeney, "Inflation and Real Growth: Some Empirical Results," *Journal of Money, Credit, and Banking*, 13 (1981), pp. 497–501.

Lohmann, Susanne, "Optimal Commitment in Monetary Policy: Credibility versus Flexibility," *American Economic Review*, 82 (1992), pp. 273–286.

McCallum, Bennett T., "Two Fallacies Concerning Central-Bank Independence," *American Economic Review*, Papers and Proceedings, 85 (1995a), pp. 207–211.

——, "Inflation Targeting in Canada, New Zealand, Sweden, the United Kingdom, and in General," Working Paper, Carnegie Mellon University, 1995b.

Marsh, David, *The Bundesbank. The Bank That Rules Europe*, London, Heinemann, 1992.

Mascaro, Angelo, and Allan H. Meltzer, "Long- and Short-Term Interest Rates in a Risky World," *Journal of Monetary Economics*, 12 (1983), pp. 485–518.

Masciandaro, Donato, and Guido Tabellini, "Monetary Regimes and Fiscal Deficits: A Comparative Analysis," in Hang-sheng Cheng, ed., *Monetary Policy in Pacific Basin Countries*, Dordrecht and Lancaster, Kluwer, 1988, pp. 125–152.

Moser, Peter, "The Supply of Central Bank Independence," Discussion Paper No. 9501, University of St. Gallen, 1994.

Mundell, Robert A., "Inflation and Real Interest," *Journal of Political Economy*, 71 (1963), pp. 280–283.

Neumann, Manfred J. M., "Precommitment by Central Bank Independence," *Open Economies Review*, 2 (1991), pp. 95–112.

Parkin, Michael, "Domestic Monetary Institutions and the Deficit," in James M. Buchanan, Charles K. Rowley, and Robert D. Tollison, eds., *Deficits*, Oxford, Blackwell, 1987, pp. 310–337.

Persson, Torsten, and Lars E.O. Svensson, "Why a Stubborn Conservative Would Run a Deficit? Policy with Time Consistent Preferences," *Quarterly Journal of Economics*, 104 (1989), pp. 325–345.

Persson, Torsten, and Guido Tabellini, "Designing Institutions for Monetary Stability," *Carnegie-Rochester Conference Series on Public Policy*, 39 (1993), pp. 53–84.

Pollard, Patricia S., "Central Bank Independence and Economic Performance," *Federal Reserve Bank of St. Louis Review*, 75 (July/August 1993), pp. 21–36.

Posen, Adam, "Why Central Bank Independence Does Not Cause Low Inflation: There Is No Institutional Fix for Politics," in Richard O'Brien, ed., *Finance and the International Economy*, Vol. 7, Oxford, Oxford University Press, 1993a.

——, "Central Banks and Politics," *Amex Bank Review*, 20 (1993b), p. 5.

———, "Central Bank Independence and Disinflationary Credibility: A Missing Link," Brookings Discussion Paper in International Economics No. 109, Washington, D.C., Brookings Institution, August 1994.

Rogoff, Kenneth, "The Optimal Degree of Commitment to an Intermediate Monetary Target," *Quarterly Journal of Economics*, 110 (1985), pp. 1169–1190.

Roll, Eric et al., "Independent and Accountable, A New Mandate for the Bank of England," report of an independent panel chaired by Eric Roll, London, Centre for Economic Policy Research, October 1993.

Sargent, Thomas J., and Neil Wallace, "Some Unpleasant Monetarist Arithmetic," *Federal Reserve Bank of Minneapolis Quarterly Review*, 5 (1981), pp. 1–17.

Schaling, Eric, *Institutions and Monetary Policy: Credibility, Flexibility and Central Bank Independence*, Aldershot, Edward Elgar, 1995.

Smith, Eric O., *The German Economy*, London, Routledge, 1994.

Svensson, Lars E.O., "Optimal Inflation Targets, Conservative Central Banks, and Linear Inflation Contracts," Working Paper, Stockholm University, 1995.

Tabellini, Guido, and Alberto Alesina, "Voting on the Budget Deficit," *American Economic Review*, 80 (1990), pp. 37–49.

Tabellini, Guido, and Vincenzo La Via, "Money, Deficit and Public Debt in the United States," *Review of Economics and Statistics*, 71 (1989), pp. 15–25.

Ungerer, Horst, "The EMS, 1979–1990, Policies-Evolution-Outlook," *Konjunkturpolitik*, 36 (1990), pp. 329–362.

Waller, Christopher J., "The Choice of a Conservative Central Banker in a Multisector Economy," *American Economic Review*, 82 (1992a), pp. 1006–1012.

———, "A Bargaining Model of Partisan Appointments to the Central Bank," *Journal of Monetary Economics*, 29 (1992b), pp. 411–428.

Walsh, Carl E., "Optimal Contracts for Independent Central Bankers: Private Information, Performance Measures and Reappointment," Working Paper No. 93–02, Federal Reserve Bank of San Francisco, 1993.

———, "Central Bank Independence and the Costs of Disinflation in the EC," in Barry Eichengreen, Jeffry Frieden, and Jürgen von Hagen, eds., *Monetary and Fiscal Policy in an Integrated Europe*, Berlin, Heidelberg, and New York, Springer-Verlag, 1995a, pp. 12–37.

———, "Optimal Contracts for Central Bankers," *American Economic Review*, 85 (1995b), pp. 150–167.

Zijlstra, Jelle, *Per Slot van Rekening*, Amsterdam, Uitgeverij Contact, 1992.

PUBLICATIONS OF THE
INTERNATIONAL FINANCE SECTION

Notice to Contributors

The International Finance Section publishes papers in four series: ESSAYS IN INTERNATIONAL FINANCE, PRINCETON STUDIES IN INTERNATIONAL FINANCE, and SPECIAL PAPERS IN INTERNATIONAL ECONOMICS contain new work not published elsewhere. REPRINTS IN INTERNATIONAL FINANCE reproduce journal articles previously published by Princeton faculty members associated with the Section. The Section welcomes the submission of manuscripts for publication under the following guidelines:

ESSAYS are meant to disseminate new views about international financial matters and should be accessible to well-informed nonspecialists as well as to professional economists. Technical terms, tables, and charts should be used sparingly; mathematics should be avoided.

STUDIES are devoted to new research on international finance, with preference given to empirical work. They should be comparable in originality and technical proficiency to papers published in leading economic journals. They should be of medium length, longer than a journal article but shorter than a book.

SPECIAL PAPERS are surveys of research on particular topics and should be suitable for use in undergraduate courses. They may be concerned with international trade as well as international finance. They should also be of medium length.

Manuscripts should be submitted in triplicate, typed single sided and double spaced throughout on 8½ by 11 white bond paper. Publication can be expedited if manuscripts are computer keyboarded in WordPerfect 5.1 or a compatible program. Additional instructions and a style guide are available from the Section.

How to Obtain Publications

The Section's publications are distributed free of charge to college, university, and public libraries and to nongovernmental, nonprofit research institutions. Eligible institutions may ask to be placed on the Section's permanent mailing list.

Individuals and institutions not qualifying for free distribution may receive all publications for the calendar year for a subscription fee of $40.00. Late subscribers will receive all back issues for the year during which they subscribe. Subscribers should notify the Section promptly of any change in address, giving the old address as well as the new.

Publications may be ordered individually, with payment made in advance. ESSAYS and REPRINTS cost $8.00 each; STUDIES and SPECIAL PAPERS cost $11.00. An additional $1.50 should be sent for postage and handling within the United States, Canada, and Mexico; $1.75 should be added for surface delivery outside the region.

All payments must be made in U.S. dollars. Subscription fees and charges for single issues will be waived for organizations and individuals in countries where foreign-exchange regulations prohibit dollar payments.

Please address all correspondence, submissions, and orders to:

International Finance Section
Department of Economics, Fisher Hall
Princeton University
Princeton, New Jersey 08544-1021

List of Recent Publications

A complete list of publications may be obtained from the International Finance Section.

ESSAYS IN INTERNATIONAL FINANCE

163. Arminio Fraga, *German Reparations and Brazilian Debt: A Comparative Study*. (July 1986)
164. Jack M. Guttentag and Richard J. Herring, *Disaster Myopia in International Banking*. (September 1986)
165. Rudiger Dornbusch, *Inflation, Exchange Rates, and Stabilization*. (October 1986)
166. John Spraos, *IMF Conditionality: Ineffectual, Inefficient, Mistargeted*. (December 1986)
167. Rainer Stefano Masera, *An Increasing Role for the ECU: A Character in Search of a Script*. (June 1987)
168. Paul Mosley, *Conditionality as Bargaining Process: Structural-Adjustment Lending, 1980-86*. (October 1987)
169. Paul A. Volcker, Ralph C. Bryant, Leonhard Gleske, Gottfried Haberler, Alexandre Lamfalussy, Shijuro Ogata, Jesús Silva-Herzog, Ross M. Starr, James Tobin, and Robert Triffin, *International Monetary Cooperation: Essays in Honor of Henry C. Wallich*. (December 1987)
170. Shafiqul Islam, *The Dollar and the Policy-Performance-Confidence Mix*. (July 1988)
171. James M. Boughton, *The Monetary Approach to Exchange Rates: What Now Remains?* (October 1988)
172. Jack M. Guttentag and Richard M. Herring, *Accounting for Losses On Sovereign Debt: Implications for New Lending*. (May 1989)
173. Benjamin J. Cohen, *Developing-Country Debt: A Middle Way*. (May 1989)
174. Jeffrey D. Sachs, *New Approaches to the Latin American Debt Crisis*. (July 1989)
175. C. David Finch, *The IMF: The Record and the Prospect*. (September 1989)
176. Graham Bird, *Loan-Loss Provisions and Third-World Debt*. (November 1989)
177. Ronald Findlay, *The "Triangular Trade" and the Atlantic Economy of the Eighteenth Century: A Simple General-Equilibrium Model*. (March 1990)
178. Alberto Giovannini, *The Transition to European Monetary Union*. (November 1990)
179. Michael L. Mussa, *Exchange Rates in Theory and in Reality*. (December 1990)
180. Warren L. Coats, Jr., Reinhard W. Furstenberg, and Peter Isard, *The SDR System and the Issue of Resource Transfers*. (December 1990)
181. George S. Tavlas, *On the International Use of Currencies: The Case of the Deutsche Mark*. (March 1991)
182. Tommaso Padoa-Schioppa, ed., with Michael Emerson, Kumiharu Shigehara, and Richard Portes, *Europe After 1992: Three Essays*. (May 1991)
183. Michael Bruno, *High Inflation and the Nominal Anchors of an Open Economy*. (June 1991)
184. Jacques J. Polak, *The Changing Nature of IMF Conditionality*. (September 1991)

185. Ethan B. Kapstein, *Supervising International Banks: Origins and Implications of the Basle Accord*. (December 1991)

186. Alessandro Giustiniani, Francesco Papadia, and Daniela Porciani, *Growth and Catch-Up in Central and Eastern Europe: Macroeconomic Effects on Western Countries*. (April 1992)

187. Michele Fratianni, Jürgen von Hagen, and Christopher Waller, *The Maastricht Way to EMU*. (June 1992)

188. Pierre-Richard Agénor, *Parallel Currency Markets in Developing Countries: Theory, Evidence, and Policy Implications*. (November 1992)

189. Beatriz Armendariz de Aghion and John Williamson, *The G-7's Joint-and-Several Blunder*. (April 1993)

190. Paul Krugman, *What Do We Need to Know About the International Monetary System?* (July 1993)

191. Peter M. Garber and Michael G. Spencer, *The Dissolution of the Austro-Hungarian Empire: Lessons for Currency Reform*. (February 1994)

192. Raymond F. Mikesell, *The Bretton Woods Debates: A Memoir*. (March 1994)

193. Graham Bird, *Economic Assistance to Low-Income Countries: Should the Link be Resurrected?* (July 1994)

194. Lorenzo Bini-Smaghi, Tommaso Padoa-Schioppa, and Francesco Papadia, *The Transition to EMU in the Maastricht Treaty*. (November 1994)

195. Ariel Buira, *Reflections on the International Monetary System*. (January 1995)

196. Shinji Takagi, *From Recipient to Donor: Japan's Official Aid Flows, 1945 to 1990 and Beyond*. (March 1995)

197. Patrick Conway, *Currency Proliferation: The Monetary Legacy of the Soviet Union*. (June 1995)

PRINCETON STUDIES IN INTERNATIONAL FINANCE

57. Stephen S. Golub, *The Current-Account Balance and the Dollar: 1977-78 and 1983-84*. (October 1986)

58. John T. Cuddington, *Capital Flight: Estimates, Issues, and Explanations*. (December 1986)

59. Vincent P. Crawford, *International Lending, Long-Term Credit Relationships, and Dynamic Contract Theory*. (March 1987)

60. Thorvaldur Gylfason, *Credit Policy and Economic Activity in Developing Countries with IMF Stabilization Programs*. (August 1987)

61. Stephen A. Schuker, *American "Reparations" to Germany, 1919-33: Implications for the Third-World Debt Crisis*. (July 1988)

62. Steven B. Kamin, *Devaluation, External Balance, and Macroeconomic Performance: A Look at the Numbers*. (August 1988)

63. Jacob A. Frenkel and Assaf Razin, *Spending, Taxes, and Deficits: International-Intertemporal Approach*. (December 1988)

64. Jeffrey A. Frankel, *Obstacles to International Macroeconomic Policy Coordination*. (December 1988)

65. Peter Hooper and Catherine L. Mann, *The Emergence and Persistence of the U.S. External Imbalance, 1980-87*. (October 1989)

66. Helmut Reisen, *Public Debt, External Competitiveness, and Fiscal Discipline in Developing Countries*. (November 1989)

67. Victor Argy, Warwick McKibbin, and Eric Siegloff, *Exchange-Rate Regimes for a Small Economy in a Multi-Country World.* (December 1989)
68. Mark Gersovitz and Christina H. Paxson, *The Economies of Africa and the Prices of Their Exports.* (October 1990)
69. Felipe Larraín and Andrés Velasco, *Can Swaps Solve the Debt Crisis? Lessons from the Chilean Experience.* (November 1990)
70. Kaushik Basu, *The International Debt Problem, Credit Rationing and Loan Pushing: Theory and Experience.* (October 1991)
71. Daniel Gros and Alfred Steinherr, *Economic Reform in the Soviet Union: Pas de Deux between Disintegration and Macroeconomic Destabilization.* (November 1991)
72. George M. von Furstenberg and Joseph P. Daniels, *Economic Summit Declarations, 1975-1989: Examining the Written Record of International Cooperation.* (February 1992)
73. Ishac Diwan and Dani Rodrik, *External Debt, Adjustment, and Burden Sharing: A Unified Framework.* (November 1992)
74. Barry Eichengreen, *Should the Maastricht Treaty Be Saved?* (December 1992)
75. Adam Klug, *The German Buybacks, 1932-1939: A Cure for Overhang?* (November 1993)
76. Tamim Bayoumi and Barry Eichengreen, *One Money or Many? Analyzing the Prospects for Monetary Unification in Various Parts of the World.* (September 1994)
77. Edward E. Leamer, *The Heckscher-Ohlin Model in Theory and Practice.* (February 1995)
78. Thorvaldur Gylfason, *The Macroeconomics of European Agriculture.* (May 1995)
79. Angus S. Deaton and Ronald I. Miller, *International Commodity Prices, Macroeconomic Performance, and Politics in Sub-Saharan Africa.* (December 1995)
80. Chander Kant, *Foreign Direct Investment and Capital Flight.* (April 1996)

SPECIAL PAPERS IN INTERNATIONAL ECONOMICS

16. Elhanan Helpman, *Monopolistic Competition in Trade Theory.* (June 1990)
17. Richard Pomfret, *International Trade Policy with Imperfect Competition.* (August 1992)
18. Hali J. Edison, *The Effectiveness of Central-Bank Intervention: A Survey of the Literature After 1982.* (July 1993)
19. Sylvester W.C. Eijffinger and Jakob de Haan, *The Political Economy of Central-Bank Independence.* (May 1996)

REPRINTS IN INTERNATIONAL FINANCE

27. Peter B. Kenen, *Transitional Arrangements for Trade and Payments Among the CMEA Countries*; reprinted from *International Monetary Fund Staff Papers* 38 (2), 1991. (July 1991)
28. Peter B. Kenen, *Ways to Reform Exchange-Rate Arrangements*; reprinted from *Bretton Woods: Looking to the Future*, 1994. (November 1994)